Authority and Leadership
in the Church

Authority and Leadership in the Church

Past Directions and Future Possibilities

by

Thomas P. Rausch, S.J.

 Michael Glazier
Wilmington Delaware

ABOUT THE AUTHOR

Rev. Thomas P. Rausch, S.J. is Professor of Theology and Rector of the Jesuit Community at Loyola Marymount University in Los Angeles. He is a member of both the Theological Commission and the Ecumenical Commission of the Archdiocese of Los Angeles. He is also a member of the Los Angeles Lutheran Roman Catholic Committee and the Los Angeles Catholic Evangelical Dialogue. Father Rausch's teaching areas include New Testament, ecclesiology, christology, and ecumenism. He is the author of *The Roots of the Catholic Tradition* (Michael Glazier, 1986) and has published in *America, The Clergy Review, Ecumenical Trends, The Irish Theological Quarterly, The Lutheran Forum, One in Christ, The Priest, Sojourners, Spirituality Today,* and *Theological Studies.*

First published in 1989 by Michael Glazier, Inc., 1935 West Fourth Street, Wilmington, Delaware 19805. ©1989 by Thomas P. Rausch. All rights reserved.

Library of Congress Cataloging-in-Publication Data

Rausch, Thomas P.
  Authority in the Church.

  Bibliography: p.
  1. Church—Authority.   2. Catholic Church—Doctrines.
I. Title.
BX1746.R37   1988   262'.8   88-24621
ISBN 0-89453-745-8

Typography by Edith Warren.
Printed in the U.S.A.

To my Jesuit brothers

Contents

Acknowledgements

I would like to acknowledge my gratitude to a number of people who have played an important part in the genesis, development, and completion of this book.

Five of the seven chapters were developed specifically for the 23rd Faith and Order Conference of the Texas Conference of Churches on the subject "Authority in the Body of Christ," November 12-14, 1987 at Mo Ranch, Hunt, Texas. I am grateful to the Texas Conference for the invitation to be one of the presenters for the 23rd Conference and especially to Garland Pohl for extending it.

John A. Coleman, S.J., of the Jesuit School of Theology, Berkeley, encouraged me to write the book on the basis of my work in preparing for the Conference.

Jeffrey Gros, F.S.C., Director of the Commission on Faith and Order for the National Council of the Churches of Christ, has been involved in the project in a number of ways and shared with me some of his own reflections from his long years of ecumenical involvement.

Walter J. Burghardt, S.J., editor of *Theological Studies,* graciously allowed me to publish here as chapter 5 a revised version of an article originally published in his journal.

Herbert J. Ryan, S.J., of the Department of Theology, Loyola Marymount University, has been over the years an important source of encouragement and help. I have always been able to count on him to review a difficult passage or to suggest some sources or approaches to unravel a particular problem. I am very grateful for his interest and support.

Finally, Michael Downey, my colleague in the Department of Theology at Loyola Marymount University, has been a great help. By his careful reading and theological critique of the work as it was in process he has contributed to both the form and the substance of this book.

To all these friends I want to express my appreciation and my deep gratitude.

Thomas P. Rausch, S.J.

Introduction

What will the church of tomorrow be like? I began thinking about this question several years ago when I was privileged to spend the better part of a sabbatical year at the Ecumenical Institute at Bossey, just outside Geneva. The Institute is a study and conference center sponsored by the World Council of Churches, and I was there as an official Roman Catholic representative.

The experience was a fascinating one. The proximity of Geneva and the intimate relationship between Bossey and the World Council of Churches helped me to gain an appreciation of the ongoing, sometimes difficult, but always challenging relationship between the WCC and the Roman Catholic Church. Living at Bossey enabled me to meet pastors and church leaders from all over the world. Especially valuable was the Bossey Graduate School, a unique program which brings together men and women, ordained and lay , from some thirty different countries and from Christian communities as different from one another as the Salvation Army and the Orthodox Churches.

For me, it was a whole new experience of church, not always familiar or comfortable, but one that was rich in possibilities for the future. From the Graduate School especially I gained some insight into what tomorrow's church might be like. It will be a world church, culturally diverse but ecumenically inclusive.[1] At the same time the experience in-

---

[1]See Karl Rahner, "Towards a Fundamental Theological Interpretation of Vatican Council II," *Theological Studies* 40 (1979) 716-27.

cluded some frustrations, a number of which were particularly instructive because they underline tensions and
unresolved problems within the ecumenical movement itself.
There was first of all the very difficult and painful question
of intercommunion. Then there were two issues which are
closely related: first, different approaches to authority in the
church, and second, an inability to realistically image the
ecumenical future.

I found this inability to talk realistically about the ecumenical future particularly frustrating. Apart from an opening
lecture on various ways of understanding Christian unity,
neither the Graduate School nor those who spoke to us from
the WCC addressed this issue. Nor did anyone raise the
question of how the ultimate relationship between the WCC
and the Roman Catholic Church might be perceived.

There is need for a good deal of creative thinking on the
part of both Geneva and Rome. Rome's emphasis on doctrinal agreement seems to have taken the form of a "max-
imalist" position that would include the whole panoply of
papal and mariological dogmas among those doctrines about
which agreement is necessary for the restoration of ecclesial
communion. And many in the WCC seem to expect that the
ecumenical problem will be solved when the Roman Catholic
Church finally allows intercommunion and agrees to become
one more church among the WCC's 300 or so member
churches. But neither of these positions is realistic.

Since returning from Bossey I have continued to reflect on
these issues. This book is an attempt to address the question
of authority in the church of tomorrow. What is the nature
of authority and how did it develop in the church? What
distinguishes Protestant and Roman Catholic approaches to
authority today? And how might authority be exercised in
tomorrow's church? Any understanding of ecclesial authority
must find its ultimate inspiration and model in the person of
Jesus, so we need to consider the way that Jesus understood
and exercised the authority that was his. The ecumenical
dialogues, which in some cases have been in existence for
almost thirty years, have led to a surprising consensus on the
nature and role of authority in the church. We will review
the more important dialogue statements. And since ecclesial

authority cannot be understood apart from its place within the whole church, we will consider the concept of reception which describes an important reality in the life of the church. Finally we will consider different models of Christian unity and attempt to suggest how authority might be renewed, reformed, and exercised in the church of tomorrow.

Some Christian churches have not yet embraced the ecumenical movement. Especially in the United States there is a very large and usually conservative group of Christians from free church, evangelical, and Pentecostal traditions who are generally neither involved nor interested in the movement for Christian unity. Recently, however, several dialogues have been initiated between some of these traditions and the mainline churches.[2] It is important for Christians from the mainline churches to hear and come to appreciate their concerns, many of which are quite legitimate. But the fact that these more conservative churches have not been actively involved in the ecumenical movement over the last thirty years means that this study will be more concerned with the mainline churches and with the consensus emerging from the dialogues in which they have been engaged.

Furthermore, because this study is the work of someone writing from within the Roman Catholic tradition it will focus on what the Roman Catholic Church brings to the ecumenical movement and how its own structures might be renewed and reformed in order to do all it can to make reconciliation possible. In light of its history, its influence, and the very authority it claims, the Roman Catholic Church has a special responsibility.

[2]See Basil Meeking and John Stott (ed.), *The Evangelical-Roman Catholic Dialogue on Mission: 1977-1984* (William B. Eerdmans/The Paternoster Press, 1986); Jerry L. Sandige, (ed.), *Roman Catholic/Pentecostal Dialogue (1977-1982): A Study in Developing Ecumenism* (New York: Peter Lang, 1987); on October 22-24, 1986 the first consultation between the National Council of Churches and representatives of the Pentecostal churches was held at Fuller Theological Seminary in Pasadena, California; for the papers, see *One in Christ*, 23 (1987) 61-156.

1

Who Speaks for the Church?

One of the unresolved ecumenical questions is that of authority. Roman Catholics in dialogue with Protestants frequently raise this question from a practical point of view; who is able to speak authoritatively for this particular church? They have the sense that in many Protestant churches teaching and decision-making authority seems too diffuse. On the other hand Protestants are not at all comfortable with the way authority is understood and exercised in the Roman Catholic Church. Though Protestants differ among themselves on the question of how authority is to be exercised, they generally agree that the Roman Catholic approach to authority is too clerical; it represents an absolutizing of hierarchical authority which disenfranchises the authority and integrity of local churches, relegates the laity to passive observance, and in the final analysis is contrary to the freedom of the Gospel.

Protestant and Catholic Approaches

Protestant theologian Robert McAfee Brown once observed that the question of authority is the "Achilles' heel" of Protestantism, for it is difficult for Protestants to answer clearly just where their ultimate authority rests and how it is exercised.[1] In the sixteenth century the Reformers substituted

[1]Robert McAfee Brown, *The Spirit of Protestantism* (New York: Oxford University Press, 1961), p. 171.

the authority of Scripture for the authority of the church. For a time the resulting principle "Scripture alone" worked well enough in the Reformation tradition. But eventually the clarity of Scripture which the Reformers had presupposed (*Scriptura sui interpres*) collapsed, undermined by the Enlightenment in the eighteenth century and the triumph of the historical critical method in the nineteenth. The resulting question of how Scripture was to be interpreted has led to what has been called a "crisis" for the scriptural principle in the twentieth century.[2]

The Reformers' approach to authority had perhaps even more profound consequences for the unity of the church. Most of the Reformers had sought to renew, not to divide, the western church, but they were unable to preserve Christian unity even within the Reformation itself. In the Europe of the sixteenth century three main traditions emerged; the Lutheran in Germany and Scandinavia, the Reformed or Calvinist in Switzerland and France, and the Anglican in England. But there was also the more radical left wing of the Reformation. Communities such as the Swiss Brethren, the Hutterites in Moravia, and the Dutch Mennonites—known collectively as the Anabaptists—argued that the church had "fallen" under Constantine and sought to restore Christian life on the model of the primitive church.

The seeds of reform, once sown, soon spread and multiplied. Calvin's thought proved especially influential, spreading to Eastern Europe, the Netherlands, Scotland, England, Ireland, and ultimately to the British colonies in North America. The other traditions also came to North America. And new reform movements like the Baptists in seventeenth century England and the Methodists in the eighteenth century continued to lead to the formation of new churches. Consider the incredible diversity of American Protestantism, with its mainline churches, evangelicals, fundamentalists, pentecostals, and various sects. Or the unwelcome divisions replicated in the "new churches" of the developing countries

---

[2]Cf. Wolfhart Pannenberg, *Basic Questions in Theology* 1 (Philadelphia: Fortress Press, 1971), ch. 2 "The Crisis of the Scripture Principle"; also Brevard Childs, *Biblical Theology in Crisis* (Philadelphia: Westminster Press, 1970).

which received together with the Gospel the historic divisions brought by the missionaries from North America or Europe. This denominational pluralism shows how far from the Reformers' original vision the Reformation has come.

The Reformers had not intended to undermine the authority of the church. They taught with authority themselves and expected their followers to conform to their teachings which they presumed were based on the Scriptures. But in holding the Bible up against the church, they began a process which eventually was to redefine the way the authority of church leaders was understood and exercised. Today one element common to all the churches stemming from the Reformation, whether governed by bishops, presbyteral boards, or the congregations themselves, is the rejection of an exclusive identification of ecclesiastical authority with ordained ministry. Certainly the sense that Roman Catholics sometimes have about a lack of focus in regard to teaching and decision-making authority in Protestant churches could be summed up by saying that they appear too democratic. They don't seem to have enough authority.

That certainly is not the case in the Roman Catholic Church, with its hierarchical structure and emphasis on episcopal teaching authority. For Roman Catholics the problem is just the reverse, not too little authority, but too much, or perhaps more accurately, an authority that is at once too centralized, too clerical, and not sufficiently accountable to those for whom it speaks. This seems to be especially true of the way the Vatican, the church's administrative bureaucracy, seeks to regulate Catholic theology and guard its own particular understanding of Catholic orthodoxy through its various congregations.

A number of examples come immediately to mind, many of them involving the Congregation for the Doctrine of the Faith (CDF).[3] Prior to 1965 the CDF was known as the Holy Office; in previous centuries it was called the Roman Inquisition. The particular responsibility of the CDF is to

---

[3]See also Patrick Granfield, *The Limits of the Papacy* (New York: Crossroad, 1987), pp. 4-31 for a careful and complete record of recent Vatican interventions.

watch over the purity of Catholic doctrine. After the Second Vatican Council the authority of the CDF was somewhat curtailed, for the Council had reversed a number of positions previously held by the Roman authorities and vindicated theologians such as Yves Congar, Henri de Lubac, Teilhard de Chardin, Karl Rahner, and the American Jesuit John Courtney Murray—the inspiration behind the Council document on religious liberty—all of whom had felt the heavy hand of the Holy Office by restrictions on their rights to teach and publish. It has now been some time since the doctrinal congregation has put suspected authors and works on the index of forbidden books. The index is gone. But the CDF has hardly been inactive. Particularly in the last eight or nine years a number of theologians have been challenged and in some cases disciplined by the congregation. Some examples...

In 1979 the Holy See withdrew Hans Küng's canonical mission or license to teach as a Catholic theologian. This was after a long correspondence between the Swiss theologian, who teaches at the University of Tübingen, and the CDF.[4] Also in 1979 the Dutch Dominican Edward Schillebeeckx had to go to Rome to explain his views on christology, expressed in his book, *Jesus: An Experiment in Christology.*[5] Following Schillebeeckx, in 1984 the Brazilian Franciscan Leonardo Boff was summoned to Rome to discuss his views on liberation theology. In 1985 Boff was "silenced," ordered not to publish or speak publicly for a period of time, a prohibition lifted in early April 1986 by Pope John Paul II not long after his meeting with the Brazilian bishops.

The most recent action of the CDF involved an American theologian, Charles Curran, a professor of moral theology at Catholic University in Washington, D.C. Curran had been ordered to retract his positions on contraception, abortion, euthanasia, masturbation, homosexuality, premarital inter-

---

[4]See *The Küng Dialogue: Facts and Documents,* (Washington: United States Catholic Conference, 1980).

[5]Edward Schillebeeckx, *Jesus: An Experiment in Christology* (New York: Crossroad, 1981).

course, and the indissolubility of marriage, all of which dissent from the teachings of the magisterium of the church, or lose his position as a professor of Catholic theology at Catholic University. After an exchange of letters with the Congregation, Curran received a letter from the head of the CDF, Cardinal Joseph Ratzinger, on August 18, 1986 stating that as one dissenting from the magisterium he was "no longer suitable nor eligible to exercise the function of a Professor of Catholic Theology."[6] The Curran case has been of such interest to the academic community in the United States that the prestigious *Chronicle of Higher Education* reported the whole story, publishing Ratzinger's letter along with a statement by Washington's Archbishop James A. Hickey together with Curran's reply.[7]

The CDF is not, however, the only Vatican congregation which has been making headlines recently in the attempt to enforce a particular vision of orthodoxy. In 1984, after 24 American nuns who had signed an open statement in the *New York Times* claiming that there exists a plurality of positions among Catholics on abortion, Cardinal Jerome Hamer, Prefect of the Congregation for Religious and Secular Institutes, demanded that they change their positions or risk dismissal from their religious communities.

Another Vatican congregation, the Congregation for Catholic Education, directed by the former Archbishop of Washington, Cardinal William Baum, has drafted a pontifical document on Catholic universities which attempts to establish a juridical relationship between the universities and their local bishops. The intent is that the bishop would have the ability to require a university to dismiss a theology professor or campus minister whose "doctrinal integrity and uprightness of life" was considered unacceptable. This reflects canon 812 of the new *Code of Canon Law* (1983) which states that Catholic theologians teaching in Catholic univer-

---

[6] *Origins* 16 (1986) 203.

[7] *Chronicle of Higher Education* 33 (September 3, 1986) 44-47; see also Charles E. Curran, *Faithful Dissent,* (Kansas City: Sheed & Ward, 1986) and *Vatican Authority and American Catholic Dissent,* ed. William W. May (New York: Crossroad, 1987).

sities must receive a "mandate" from a competent ecclesiastical authority.[8]

This recent effort to redefine the relationship between the hierarchy and private Catholic universities has alarmed both university administrators and faculty members in the United States.[9] Many Catholic professors see a "sword of Damocles" hanging over their heads, threatening their academic freedom and even their positions. Catholic university presidents worry over the loss of the autonomy of their institutions, and with that, the loss of government financial assistance. Some express the fear that Catholic theologians will leave their schools and seek positions at non-Catholic institutions in order to safeguard their academic freedom.

Finally, in what represents the most alarming intervention, on September 3, 1986, Seattle's Archbishop Raymond Hunthausen confirmed in a letter to his priests that he had been required by the Vatican to turn over to his auxiliary, Bishop Donald Wuerl, complete and final decision-making power in the areas of the archdiocesan marriage tribunal, liturgy, formation of seminarians, and continuing education of priests, as well as in respect to priests leaving the ministry and laicized clergy. An official of the Congregation for Bishops described the action as "disciplinary," meant to correct an extraordinary situation. There are few precedents for such an intervention in the life of a local church. Msgr. John Tracy Ellis has observed that there have been some in the past in the United States, but according to his recollection only in cases where a bishop had severe financial problems or was considered incompetent because of age.[10] This case has since been settled amicably through the efforts of a committee of three U.S. bishops who reviewed the situation and made recommendations to Rome for its solution.

However these recent examples of the exercise of authority in the Roman Catholic Church, though important for the

[8]See Ladislas Orsy, "The Mandate to Teach Theological Disciplines: Glosses on Canon 812 of the New Code," *Theological Studies* 44 (1983) 476-488.

[9]See William Cenkner, "Theology and the Magisterium: What does Athens Have to Say to Jerusalem?" in *Current Issues in Catholic Higher Education* 7 (1987) 9-12.

[10]*National Catholic Reporter*, (September 12, 1986) 5.

Catholic Church in the United States, do not voice the most basic question. They concern the relation between the center, Rome, and local or regional churches. There will inevitably be tensions here as the worldwide Catholic Church-following the Second Vatican Council—learns to understand itself and live, not as a monolithic institution governed by a central administration under the pope, but as a communion of churches in communion with the bishop of Rome.[11]

Critical Questions for Contemporary Catholicism

Much more critical today is the question of how teaching and decision-making authority in matters effecting the entire Church is exercised. As it approaches the twenty-first century, the Roman Catholic Church faces a number of issues which may well prove crucial for its future. Even to raise these issues, among them priestly celibacy, the role of women, and church teaching in the area of sexuality and marriage, is to touch raw nerves; people become uncomfortable, pulse rates and voices are raised, and the deep polarization which exists in the church emerges into focus. In a sense these are inner-ecclesial issues. It could be argued that they do not address the deeper issues that confront all believers today, the growing gap between the rich and the poor, human rights and social justice, the management of the environment, even the survival of humanity itself. But because they affect both the individual's relation to the church and the church's ability to minister to its members and to the world they are vital. Here also emerges the most basic question: who speaks for church? Let us consider briefly some of these issues.

Celibacy. Although celibacy is a Gospel value, its connection with the church's ordained ministry is not intrinsic. It did not become mandatory for clergy in the western church until 1139, despite a number of earlier efforts to require it. In

[11]See J.M.R. Tillard, *The Bishop of Rome* (Wilmington, Delaware: Michael Glazier, 1983), pp. 34-41; also Vatican II, *Dogmatic Constitution on the Church* (LG), no. 26 in *The Documents of Vatican II*, ed. Walter M. Abbott (New York: the America Press, 1966), pp. 50-51.

the sixteenth century celibacy surfaced as an issue in the Reformation. It was one of the tragedies of church history that the Lutheran and Catholic theologians who met at Augsburg in July of 1530 in an effort to bring the two sides together were able to reach agreement on the most serious theological controversies which had previously divided them, but ultimately, the negotiations foundered. The two sides were unable to reach agreement on giving the chalice to the laity, on monastic vows, on the difficult question of the restoration of church property which had changed hands in the previous years, and on the marriage of priests.[12]

Today celibacy reappears as a cause (though not the only one) in the growing shortage of priests throughout the Roman Catholic Church. The situation is bad in the United States, where the number of active priests decreased by 16 percent during the 70s, while the number of seminarians decreased by almost 25,000. According to figures released in November, 1987, the total number of seminarians in the United States dropped below 10,000.[13]

The situation is worse in Europe, where the number of ordinations has been decreasing over the years. France had 950 ordinations in 1952, and only 99 in 1977. Because of the shortage of priests, some 1,500 French parishes are not able to have a Sunday Eucharist; instead they celebrate lay-led communion services. There are severe shortages in Germany, the Netherlands, Belgium, even in Portugal and southern Spain. In Germany some dioceses have as many as 40 percent of their parishes without a resident priest.

In Latin America, Africa, and Asia the shortage of priests is critical. Based on figures from the official *Annuarium Statisticum Ecclesiae* for 1976 it has been estimated that about 50 percent of the parishes and mission stations in the Third World lack a resident priest; many of these are com-

---

[12]Melanchthon, the author of the Augsburg Confession, was ready to make concessions, even to acknowledge the jurisdiction of the bishops, if only Rome would concede the chalice to the laity and a married clergy. See Erwin Iserloh, "Die Confessio Augustana als Anfrage an Lutheraner und Katholiken im 16. Jahrhundert und Heute," *Catholica* 33 (1979) 32.

[13]Figures compiled by the Center for Applied Research on the Apostolate, cited in *The National Catholic Reporter* 24 (November 13, 1987) 3.

munities of thousands of baptized Catholics who are thus denied regular access to the sacraments. The situation is complicated in Latin American countries like Bolivia, Brazil Ecuador, Peru, and Venezuela which are heavily dependent on foreign, religious order priests, most of them from the countries of Europe, especially Spain, which are themselves suffering from a constantly diminishing number of religious vocations.[14] In 1982 the ratio of priests to Catholic population for North America was 1 to 886; in Latin America it was 1 to 6,911, and in Africa it was 1 to 17,233. In Brazil, the world's largest Catholic region, the ratio is 1 to 9,000.[15] And as the number of priests continues to decrease, the Catholic population in these countries continues to grow. In a recent survey of the priest shortage in the Roman Catholic Church, Dean Hoge points out that the recent reports of an increase in vocations in the Third World will not change significantly the widening gap in the ratio of priests to Catholic populations because of the continued growth in the number of Catholics.[16] Hoge argues that the vocation crisis is not the result of a lack of spiritual vitality or a loss of faith in the Catholic Church; the research he examines suggests rather that it is "largely a matter of institutional policies."[17]

One consequence of the worldwide shortage of priests is that the Catholic Church is increasingly being forced to choose between its present requirements for ordination and its tradition of eucharistic worship. As sociologist and theologian John Coleman has asked, "Just who are the real traditionalists? Those who defend no options to celibacy even when it means defining Catholic communities by something other than the Eucharist or those who assume that Eucharist is more central to the Catholic imagination of ministry than

[14]Statistical data can be found in Jan Kerkhofs, "From Frustration to Liberation?" in *Minister? Pastor? Prophet? Grass-roots leadership in the churches,* Lucas Grollenberg et. al. (New York: Crossroad, 1981), pp. 5-12.

[15]Data compiled by Robert Sherry, "Shortage? What Vocation Shortage?" in *The Priest* 41 (1985) 29-31; he notes that the ratio in the United States has changed as follows: 1965:1/704; 1975: 1/791; 1983: 1/900; p. 29.

[16]Dean Hoge, *Future of Catholic Leadership: Responses to the Priest Shortage,* (Kansas City: Sheed & Ward, 1987), p. 15.

any disciplinary condition for ordination?"[18]

A related problem is the thousands of baptized Catholics in Latin America who are joining evangelical or pentecostal churches. Bonaventura Kloppenburg, a Brazilian bishop, has asserted that Latin America today is becoming Protestant at a rate faster than Central Europe did in the 16th century.[19] When representatives of the evangelical churches are challenged about what to Roman Catholics appears as an unecumenical proselytizing, they frequently respond that what is happening is not so much the result of proselytizing on the part of the evangelicals as it is the inability of the Roman Catholic Church to pastor those it has baptized because of its shortage of priests. They argue that many Latin American Catholics have been "sacramentalized but not evangelized." Without the obligation of clerical celibacy and with far less formal educational requirements for their pastors, the evangelical churches have pastors in abundance. But for the Catholic Church in Latin America, the disproportionate ratio of priests to people (in 1982 the ratio was 1 to 6,911, and specifically in Brazil, 1 to 9,000) makes effective evangelization difficult even with the emerging lay ministries.

Finally, there is the challenge presented by the growing number of small Christian communities pastored by lay people—the *comunidades eclesiales de base* or base ecclesial communities of Latin America,[20] the thousands of communities of African Catholics led by lay catechists,[21] the alternative communities in some first world countries like the United States.[22] These base communities represent a new way of being church. But because they are led by lay "co-

---

[17]Ibid., p. 18.

[18]John Coleman, "The Future of Ministry," *America* 144 (1981) 248-49.

[19]Cited in Thomas H. Stahel, "The Sects in Paraguay," *America* 155 (1986) 139.

[20]Cf. Leonardo Boff, *Ecclesiogenesis: the Base Communities Reinvent the Church* (Maryknoll, New York: Orbis Books, 1986).

[21]Raymond Hickey, The Case for an Auxiliary Priesthood (Maryknoll, New York: Orbis Books, 1982); see also Michel Bavarel, *New Communities, New Ministries* (Maryknoll, New York: Orbis Books, 1983).

[22]See Karl Rahner, *The Shape of the Church to Come* (New York: Seabury Press, 1974), pp. 108-118.

ordinators" they are not able to celebrate the Eucharist. Yet as they continue to gather for reflection on Scripture, for prayer, and action on behalf of the community, the question of Eucharist is bound to arise. Some of the more radical alternative women's communities such as women-church[23] are already celebrating their own communion liturgies. Some of these base communities could be a source of future divisions.

Thus the basic issue is not simply celibacy, but the broader question of who can be ordained. Leonardo Boff argues that "to deprive thousands upon thousands of communities of the sacrament of the Eucharist, and of the incomparable benefits of having an ordained minister, through inflexibility in maintaining a tradition that has bound a necessary service (that of priesthood) to a free charism (that of celibacy) is tantamount to an unlawful violation of the rights of the faithful."[24] Little wonder that Boff is not popular in Rome! But others have also pointed out that in the early church a situation in which a community was unable to celebrate the Eucharist for want of an ordained leader was unthinkable. A community would always choose a community member with a charism for leadership as presider who would then be ordained with the help of the bishops of the neighboring churches.[25] Boff calls for an extraordinary solution in light of an extraordinary situation, the recognition of extraordinary ministers to celebrate the Lord's Supper as a true eucharistic sacrament, even though he suggests distinguishing it from the canonical Mass.[26]

Women in the Church. One of the most critical and potentially explosive questions facing the Catholic Church in the United States today is that of the role of women. There are actually two issues here, first of all, the broad question of

---

[23]See Rosemary Ruether, *Women-Church* (San Francisco: Harper and Row, 1986).

[24]Boff, *Ecclesiogenesis,* p. 63

[25]See Hervé-Marie Legrand, "The Presidency of the Eucharist According to the Ancient Tradition," *Worship* 53 (1979) 437.

[26]Boff, *Ecclesiogenesis,* pp. 70-73.

opening to women ministerial and leadership roles previously denied them, and second, the much more specific question of the ordination of women.

In response to the first question, it must be honestly admitted that the institutional church has been glacially slow to acknowledge women as equals to men and to fully recognize their gifts. Before the Second Vatican Council a double standard applied to religious women who, unlike priests, were often forbidden to dine in a restaurant, go to a movie, drive an automobile, or visit a friend's home. Such rules and "customs," it was maintained paternalistically, were for the sisters' own protection and good.

One thinks also of the thousands of sisters sent to teach huge classes of children in parochial schools without adequate preparation, sisters who spent countless vacation periods in summer schools, just to complete their undergraduate degrees. Or of their congregations, governed by rules and a canonical discipline formulated by men without representation on the part of the governed. There were no women as members of any of the 14 study groups comprising the recent Pontifical Commission for the revision of the Code of Canon Law,[27] a revision which could have considerable effect on the lives of religious women. And what can be said about religious women can be said just as well for lay women, married and single. For centuries women maintained the sanctuaries of Catholic churches but were not permitted to perform any liturgical function within them.

Today all that is changing. In many ways the role and status of women in the church have already changed, not only as a result of Vatican II, but perhaps even more because of the wider cultural changes which have affected the role and status of women in society at large. On the parish and diocesan levels, on university and seminary faculties of theology, and in ministries of all kinds women are moving into positions of responsibility and leadership previously closed to them. There are clear signs of progress, at least in some

[27]Thomas J. Green, "The Revision of Canon Law: Theological Implication," *Theological Studies* 40 (1979) 679.

areas. But there are other areas where little has changed. The new Code of Canon Law (1983) does not allow women to be installed in the ministries of lector and acolyte (can. 230). And the church still refuses to let girls function as altar servers. Such restrictive laws and practices continue to deeply offend women committed to the church. Issues such as these were raised at the 1987 Synod on the Laity in Rome, but apparently without any observable results.

What about the much more specific question of the ordination of women? Not many theologians have been convinced by the theological arguments which have been advanced by the Roman Catholic Church *against* the ordination of women.[28] And increasingly, various statistical polls show that the tide of popular opinion is shifting *toward* acceptance of the ministry of ordained women. This is not true everywhere. It will probably be a long time before African Catholics will be able to recognize women in pastoral roles of leadership, given the place of women in African society in general. Yet in other countries women are being accepted in roles which previously have been closed to them. In some third world countries where the diminishing number of priests has become critical, women are instructing and baptizing candidates, leading small groups at prayer, preaching and distributing the Eucharist, and burying the dead. The emergence of women as natural leaders or coordinators in the base communities of Latin America signals that the traditional attitudes towards women are beginning to change at least in that part of the world. In the majority of the Reformation churches the ministry of ordained women is taken for granted. At the same time there is a growing acceptance of the idea of women priests within the Catholic Church. Thus the issue will not go away. It must ultimately be faced.

Sexuality and Marriage. Nowhere is the pluralism within contemporary Roman Catholicism more evident that in regard to sexuality and marriage. Until very recent times Church teaching on these matters was virtually unquestioned.

---

[28]See *Women Priests: A Catholic Commentary on the Vatican Declaration* ed. Leonard Swidler and Arlene Swidler (New York: Paulist Press, 1977).

Failings in the area of sex were always considered seriously sinful; there was no "parvity of matter" where sex was concerned. Annulments were relatively rare and difficult to obtain. One had to apply to Rome. Catholics who divorced and remarried without an annulment were frequently ostracized by family and friends. Much the same was true for priests and nuns who "left" their vocations. No Catholic would have thought of defending—in public at least—that masturbation, premarital (or preceremonial) sex, homosexual acts, or abortion might in certain cases be legitimate options. Catholic manuals of moral theology reprinted as late as the 1960s exhaustively listed all possible sexual sins; even watching animals mate could be serious matter, though lessened if no sexual pleasure was caused.[29]

The watershed was Pope Paul VI's encyclical *Humanae vitae*, with its condemnation of artificial contraception. It was not the only cause of the shift that followed; the so-called "sexual revolution" was in full swing. But afterwards things were never the same. Social mores as well as attitudes towards church authority began to change. The number of annulments began to change dramatically. In 1969 there were 700 annulments granted to U.S. Catholics. By 1979 the number had risen to 28,000, and by 1981 it had climbed to 48,000. Theologians began to dissent publicly, and not just on the issue of contraception. Dignity, a national organization for gay and lesbian Catholics, was founded in 1969. The 1975 Vatican statement on sexual ethics was an attempt to reassert traditional church teachings, but only seemed to fuel the debate.[30] In 1977 the Catholic Theological Society of America published a report entitled, *Human Sexuality: New Directions in American Catholic Thought.*[31] Basically the

---

[29]For example, see Heribert Jone, *Moral Theology,* trans. and adapted by Urban Adelman (Westminster, MD: Newman Press, 1962), p. 156.

[30]Congregation for the Doctrine of the Faith, *Declaration on Certain Questions Concerning Sexual Ethics* (Washington: USCC, 1976); for responses see Richard A. McCormick, "Notes on Moral Theology: 1976," *Theological Studies* 38 (1977) 100-114.

[31]Anthony Kosnik et. al, *Human Sexuality: New Directions in American Catholic Thought* (New York: Paulist Press, 1977).

book argued for a shift from a unitive-procreative to a creative-integrative understanding of human sexuality. This meant that the link between sexual acts and procreation was no longer seen as essential. At the same time, a corresponding shift from an act-centered to a person-centered morality enabled the authors to argue for a nuanced acceptance of extra-marital and homosexual acts. Under the influence of the feminist movement some Catholics in the 80s have argued for abortion as an issue of women's reproductive rights. Feminist speakers frequently link official Catholic teaching against homosexuality, abortion, and the ordination of women as similar ideological expressions of a patriarchal church, fearful of sexuality and unable to deal with women as responsible moral agents.

Authority and Dissent

We have reviewed some of the issues presently troubling the church because they illustrate the tensions that exist within the contemporary Catholic community. The church is divided between those who understand Vatican II as the point of departure for an ongoing ecclesial renewal and those who see it as an end point, the final arbiter and standard for the renewal currently taking place. Many of these issues are rooted in immediate needs. How to provide for the liturgical and sacramental life of Catholic communities as the number of traditional sacramental ministers declines? How to give expression to a new desire for ecclesial ministry and shared responsibility on the part of people in the church presently excluded from ordination and still attract candidates to the ordained ministry? The church needs to address the issues raised by women, homosexuals, and other marginalized groups without uncritically accepting all the demands of their respective advocates.

Too many on both sides are locked into an all-or-nothing mentality. The church needs to deal more seriously with the question of the prevention of pregnancy due to rape and incest without simply abandoning its traditional position on abortion. Similarly it needs to find a way to preserve its commitment to the indissolubility of marriage and at the same time deal realistically and pastorally with the thousands of Catholics who are divorced and remarried "outside the church," without simply sanctioning divorce. The present multiplication of the number of annulments does not seem to be the answer.

Bishops as pastors should be in touch with all the members of their communities, listening to their concerns and not making the mistake of immediately identifying official pronouncements of ecclesiastical authorities with the deposit of faith. Theologians need to be able to probe the tradition, seeking new answers. Both bishops and theologians must work together, each respecting the proper competence of the other.[32]

Some, however, feel that cooperation is no longer possible because the institutional church is unwilling to change. Their critique of authority is much more radical, because without necessarily rejecting the institutional church they are challenging the principle of hierarchical authority itself. Rosemary Ruether expressed this viewpoint in a 1985 keynote address to the Call to Action annual assembly in Chicago:

> When it is evident that the existing institutional church has put insurmountable obstacles in the way of even beginning to ask, much less answer, these questions, then we should invent new vehicles of spiritual community and ministry, although the first line of exploration should be how to make use of existing ones. I believe that we are empowered by the Holy Spirit, as the people of God, to create for ourselves the expressions of worshipping community and ministry that we need, and this power cannot be alienated from us by any ecclesiastical hierarchy.[33]

Having specifically raised the question of power, Ruether calls for a "reappropriation of the ministry of word and

---

[32]See Avery Dulles, "The Two Magisteria: An Interim Reflection," in his *A Church to Believe In* (New York: Crossroad, 1982), pp. 118-132.

[33]Rosemary Radford Ruether, "Crises and Challenges of Catholicism Today," *America* 154 (1986) 157.

sacrament and service alienated from the people by an ecclesiastical ruling class."[34] In doing so she has suggested an understanding of power and authority in the church quite different from that with which most Catholic Christians are familiar. There are a number of paradigms or models of church authority operative today, consciously or unconsciously, reflecting profound differences in the Catholic theological imagination. Since our imaginations far more than our doctrines condition the way we perceive and interpret our world, we need to consider these different models of authority more carefully.

Models of Church Authority

A Christian community is organized and structured in terms of its understanding of authority. Who presides at worship, how decisions effecting the entire community are made, who has the right to speak for the church—these are all questions of how authority is understood and exercised. But the model of authority operative also has further theological implications; over a long period of time it can also determine how a community understands the nature of God, Christ, church, ministry, revelation, sacramental efficacy, and its own relation to other churches.

1. *Authority as Hierarchical.* The word "hierarchy," from the Greek words *hiereus* (priest) and *arche* (rule, principle), means literally "priest-rule." The Roman Catholic Church understands itself as having a hierarchical structure, that is, within the community of the baptized there is a divinely established authority and ordained ministry. The Council of Trent declared: "Whoever says that there is in the Catholic Church no hierarchy established by divine ordinance, consisting of bishops, presbyters, and deacons, let him be anathema" (D. 966; cf. 960). Vatican II, more sensitive to the complexities of history, softened the statement considerably, predicating divine institution only of the "ecclesiastical

[34]Ibid.

ministry" itself, and noting that this ministry has been "exercised on different levels by those who from antiquity have been called bishops, priests, and deacons" (LG 28).[35] This hierarchical authority is rooted in sacramental ordination and the principle of apostolic succession; the office entrusted by Christ to the apostles is continued by the bishops who by divine institution succeed to the place of the apostles as shepherds of the church (LG 20).

The tendency with a hierarchical model—typical of the Roman Catholic Church since the 16th century—is to identify authority exclusively with the ordained ministry, and thus with the institutional church.[36] Vatican II took a number of steps towards reversing this tendency, complementing its hierarchical understanding of authority by situating it within a less institutional ecclesiology. First of all, it reclaimed the biblical image of the church as the People of God, treating the church under this aspect in Chapter II of the *Constitution on the Church* (LG) before turning to a consideration of "The Hierarchical Structure of the Church" in Chapter III.

Secondly, it recovered the charismatic element, stressing the importance of the charismatic gifts along side the hierarchical (LG 4; cf., 7, 12). Finally the Council taught that the laity also are "in their own way made sharers in the priestly, prophetic, and kingly functions of Christ" (LG 31). Whereas previous church documents had tended to speak of the lay apostolate or "Catholic Action" as "the collaboration of the laity in the apostolate of the hierarchy" (*Decree on the Laity* 20), the *Constitution on the Church* emphasized that lay persons share in the mission of the church through their baptism and confirmation and "can also be called in various ways to a more direct form of cooperation in the apostolate of the hierarchy. . . . [and] have the capacity to be deputed by the hierarchy to exercise certain church functions for a

[35]*Lumen gentium* no. 28, in Abbott, p. 53; see Hans Küng's commentary on the differences between Trent and Vatican II on this point in his *The Church* (New York: Sheed and Ward, 1967), p. 418.

[36]See Avery Dulles, "Institution and Charism in the Church" in his *A Church to Believe In*, pp. 19-40; also "The Church as Institution" in *Models of the Church* (Garden City, New York: Doubleday & Company, 1974), pp. 31-42.

spiritual purpose" (LG 33). Still the hierarchical orientation of the Constitution is evident throughout: this same section speaks of "the distinction which the Lord made between sacred ministers and the rest of the People of God" and describes their ministry as being exercised "by teaching, by sanctifying, and by ruling with the authority of Christ" (LG 32).

One shortcoming of the hierarchical model is that it too easily assigns all authority to the ordained, thus overlooking or eliminating the other charisms and ministries. At times this has led to what Leonardo Boff identifies as a "pathological view of the Church's reality" which reduces lay persons to mere spectators in the life of the church.[37] Boff quotes two popes, one of them a canonized saint, as illustrations. Gregory XVI (1831-46) emphasized the distinction between clergy and laity: "No one can deny that the Church is an unequal society in which God destined some to be governors and others to be servants. The latter are the laity; the former, the clergy." The second, St. Pius X, said the following: "Only the college of pastors have the right and authority to lead and govern. The masses have no right and authority except that of being governed, like an obedient flock that follows its shepherd."[38] Thus the hierarchical model tends to disenfranchise lay persons; furthermore, as feminist theologians have observed, it evidences a strong patriarchial bias.

A second shortcoming is the tendency to translate this exclusivist understanding of authority into a concept of power. Ordained ministers are seen as having a special ontological power to consecrate, forgive, and bless which is not enjoyed by other Christians. Influenced by Augustine's emphasis on the efficacy of the sacraments even when celebrated by unworthy ministers and by the concept of hierarchy in the thought of Pseudo-Dionysius, medieval theology in the west increasingly lost sight of the symbolic nature of sacramentality while it stressed the power given to ordained ministers.[39]

[37]Leonardo Boff, *Church: Charism and Power*, pp. 141-142.

[38]Ibid, p. 142.

[39]See David N. Power, *Unsearchable Riches: the Symbolic Nature of Liturgy* (New York: Pueblo, 1984), pp. 48-57.

The result was a mechanistic understanding of sacramental causality which emphasized the ritual and hierarchical elements; sacraments conferred grace by the correct and valid performance of the rite. A correlative of this emphasis on ritual and hierarchical correctness was the inability to recognize the reality or validity of sacraments celebrated by ministers whose ordinations did not meet the requirements of ecclesiastical validity, i.e., those outside the apostolic succession of the historic episcopate.

Something similar happened in the area of teaching authority. The charism of apostolic teaching authority, recognized from the beginning and exercised over the centuries by the bishops, has frequently been understood, not as an office through which the faith entrusted to the entire church comes to expression, but as a special power to teach without error, possessed by all the bishops or by the pope alone. Consider the misapprehensions many Catholics have about papal infallibility.

In the popular imagination too much emphasis on a hierarchial model of authority has frequently led to a magical concept of church and sacrament. All authority is exercised by those incorporated into the hierarchical leadership through ordination in the apostolic succession. Sacraments (excluding baptism) celebrated by those not so incorporated are not recognized as sacraments, nor are their churches to be considered true churches. The truth of God's revelation in Christ does not emerge out of the community of faith but is transmitted in propositions authoritatively defined by the hierarchical magisterium.

2. *Authority as Charismatic.* A second model of authority is charismatic, stressing all authority as rooted in the Spirit given in baptism. The word charism, generally translated as "spiritual gift," comes from St. Paul who in 1 Corinthians stresses a diversity of gifts (*charismata*) and ministries (*diakonia*) within the church. While Catholic theology since the 16th century has tended to emphasize the hierarchical structure of the church, Protestant theology tends to stress the charismatic. The two emphases are not in contradiction. But as Avery Dulles has illustrated, Protestant liberalism

through the work of theologians such as Auguste Sabatier, Rudolf Sohm, and Emil Brunner has developed a theology of authority and church which makes the charismatic alone normative.[40] The original church is described as a community of disciples without formal authorities or institutional structure. The later development of ecclesiastical institutions, offices, dogmas, and official sacraments is seen as a decline.

A number of Roman Catholic theologians have been influenced by this stress on the charismatic structure of the original church. Hans Küng has adopted it in his ecclesiology to a considerable degree. He speaks of "the fundamental charismatic structure of the church,"[41] its original Pauline constitution or charismatic ordering—without appointed ministries—which must remain open as a possibility even today.[42] Gotthold Hasenhüttl, once a disciple of Küng, argues that the primitive Christian community adopted institutional forms to meet particular situations, but later these became structures of domination.[43] And Leonardo Boff stresses the charismatic structure of the primitive community, in which all shared equally in the Spirit to develop his "laical" model of church. Using Marxist categories, he argues that the church has imitated the tendency of ruling classes to appropriate all power for personal use. Over the years there has been "a gradual expropriation of the means of religious production from the Christian people by the clergy. In the early years, the Christian people as a whole shared in the power of the church, in decisions, in the choosing of ministers; later they were simply consulted; finally, in terms of power, they were totally marginalized, dispossessed of their power."[44]

Feminist theologians especially have argued for a charismatic rather than a hierarchical understanding of authority

---

[40]See Dulles, *A Church to Believe In*, p. 23.

[41]Küng, *The Church*, p. 190

[42]Ibid., p. 442.

[43]Gotthold Hasenhüttl, "Church and Institution," in *The Church as Institution*, (*Concilium*, Vol. 91), ed. Gregory Baum and Andrew Greeley (New York: Herder and Herder, 1974), pp. 11-21.

[44]Leonardo Boff, *Church: Charism and Power*, (New York: Crossroad, 1985), pp. 112-113.

in the period of Christian origins, with obvious implications
for the church today. Elisabeth Schüssler Fiorenza roots the
church in what she describes as "the Jesus movement," a
"discipleship of equals."[45] The "egalitarian" spirit of the first
disciples was continued in the early Christian missionary
movement and communities, though the equal access of men
and women to the roles of authority which it supported soon
gave way to a restrictive patriarchical leadership based on
the male heads of households.[46] Sandra Schneiders also uses
egalitarian imagery in describing the early Christian community; she speaks of "evangelical equality" as the principle
of relationships within the church.[47] Noting that it is increasingly the case that people are led to sacramental occasions
for reconciliation, Eucharist, and the anointing of the sick by
non-ordained ministers who can not celebrate them, she raises
the question of whether the need for an ordained minister in
these cases is always necessary.[48] Some women go further
and ask if ordination in the traditional sense of setting a
person apart for sacramental ministry is needed at all.[49] Joan
Campbell argues that the ecumenical movement needs to be
renewed "with models of ecumenism that are decentralized
and non-hierarchical."[50]

It is precisely the thought of incorporating women into the
hierarchy and thus reinforcing the hierarchical principle
which leads some feminists to at least question whether the
ordination of women would help bring about the type of
ecclesial renewal they seek. Sandra Schneiders summarizes
their concerns:

[45]Elisabeth Schüssler Fiorenza, *In Memory of Her*, (New York: Crossroad, 1983),
pp. 107 ff.

[46]Ibid., pp. 286-287.

[47]Sandra M. Schneiders, "Evangelical Equality," *Spirituality Today* 38 (1986)
293-302.

[48]Schneiders, "Ministry and Ordination, I, " *The Way* 20 (1980) 296.

[49]See Letty Russell, "Unity and Renewal in Feminist Perspective," *Ecumenical
Trends* 16 (1987) 190; Una M. Kroll, "Beyond the Ordination Issue," *The
Ecumenical Review,* 40 (1985) 57-65.

[50]Joan B. Campbell, "What is the Ecumenical Agenda?" *Ecumenical Trends* 16
(1987) 15.

The most problematic [ambiguity] is that ordaining women into the present structure would constitute a re-affirmation of the clerical-lay dichotomy which is a major obstacle to the development and recognition of the plurality of ministries needed in the contemporary Church. It would also retard the reexamination of the relationship between ordination and Eucharistic presidency. Finally, it might well reinforce the dysfunctional understanding of ordination as access to sacramental and political power within the Church rather than as designation for community service.[51]

What emerges from this charismatic understanding of authority and ministry is an egalitarian view of the church.[52] The church is seen as a community of equal disciples which should rid itself of structures derived from cultural or political models. Ordained ministry is not necessarily rejected, but ordained ministers are understood as doing by profession what others can and should be able to do also. Preaching and sacramental celebration should not be reserved to a small, clericalized group. What is important is competence or charism rather than office or ordination.[53] This goes beyond what George Lindbeck once called "the Reformation's thoroughly functional doctrine of the ministry," a view which holds that all Christians are able to celebrate the sacraments with full validity, though for the sake of good harmony, "all things should be done decently and in good order (1 Cor. 14:20)."[54]

Within an egalitarian framework church authorities—like civil servants—may be regarded as necessary for good government, but they share in the church's teaching office like all others, without requiring any special charism beyond

[51] Sandra M. Schneiders, "Ministry and Ordination II," *The Way* 21 (1981) 148.

[52] Cf. Denise Lardner Carmody and John Tully Carmody, *Bonded in Christ's Love* (New York: Paulist Press, 1986), pp. 202-207.

[53] Cf. John A. Coleman, "The Future of Ministry," *America* 144 (1981) 243-249.

[54] George Lindbeck, "Karl Rahner and a Protestant View of the Sacramentality of the Ministry," in the *Proceedings of the Catholic Theological Society of America* 21 (1966) 275-276.

their professional training and personal competence.

Finally this egalitarian approach is consistent with a contemporary understanding of sacramentality. The controlling insight here is that sacraments mediate grace by symbolizing. Therefore what is important is a concern for symbolic expression and a recovery of appropriate celebration rather than any concept of a received sacramental power. Sacramental efficacy is understood in terms of symbolic causality.

3. *Authority as Pluralistic.* Avery Dulles has proposed a third, pluralistic model of authority. Recognizing that authority can only teach what the whole church believes, he places primary emphasis on the general sense of the faithful- with the important qualification that the views of "committed Christians should be given more weight than those of indifferent or marginal Christians," even though the views of the latter should also be considered.[55] Then there are those who speak with special authority. First, the professional theologians or doctors have an authority based on their competence or scholarship. Secondly, there must always be room for prophetic voices in the church, men and women who can help the church to discern the truth through prophetic insight. Finally, the bishops speak with an authority based on their appointment to the church's pastoral office, assisted by the graces particular to it. In this way according to Dulles the church today can again recognize the doctoral, prophetic, and pastoral ministries present within it since biblical times.[56]

Conclusions

Authority is an issue today both within the Roman Catholic Church and for all the churches as they seek to restore the bonds of communion which have been lost historically. It continues to be an issue for the church of tomorrow. How will authority in tomorrow's church be understood and

[55]Avery Dulles, *The Resilient Church*, (Garden City, New York: Doubleday & Company, 1977), p. 100.

[56]Ibid., pp. 100-101.

exercised? Catholicism has tended to emphasize the hierarchical nature of authority while Protestantism has generally been identified with the charismatic. While some propose democratic, egalitarian models for the future, others emphasize the need for clear structures of centralized authority to safeguard Christian unity and to help the church proclaim the Gospel with a united voice.

A pluralistic model of authority recognizes the importance of both hierarchical and charismatic approaches. An overemphasis on either can easily lead to an ideology which ignores the fundamental nature of authority in the Christian community and its development in the church. It is to these issues that we now turn.

2

Jesus and Authority

Authority and Power

What is authority? The English word authority is derived from the Latin *auctor*, author; just as an author brings something into being, so a person possessing authority can bring about some effect, whether of persuasion, definition, or compliance. Thus authority conveys the idea of an ability or power to persuade, determine, command, or even exact obedience.

From a religious perspective, the ultimate source of all authority is God. Some people have a personal, moral, or charismatic authority; they are recognized as authorities by virtue of their personality, prominence, influence, or personal gifts. This is *de facto* authority. Others have an authority given to them by law or office. This is a *de jure* or juridical authority. A policeman has *de jure* authority; a famous scholar has authority *de facto*. Books, institutions, and law codes are also said to have authority.

Though authority frequently implies power, authority is not the same thing as power. Power describes the ability to compel others to do something, whether legitimately or not. People who exercise authority *de jure* generally have the power to enforce their authority. A terrorist or skyjacker with captives has power but not authority. A community has a moral authority, rooted in the influence of its founder or in its organizing vision, but if it succeeds in institutionalizing itself it generally develops structures of authority, administration, and government which include power. Because of the power inherent in their structures of authority institutions are always capable of the abuse of authority.

The church, which is both a community and an institution, is no exception here. History is replete with examples of the abuse of authority in the church. Some argue that power has no place in the church. According to John McKenzie, power is excluded because authority in the church is a function of love: "Love is the supreme motivation both of the officers and of the other members of the Church; with this motivation, anything like a power structure is forever excluded from the Church. Love is the only power which the New Testament knows."[1] Others recognize that authority and the power which authority sometimes implies is as necessary in the church as it is in other institutions.[2] The real issues are how authority is exercised in the church and the kind of community it contributes to and, most of all, whether it finds its foundation in the authority of Jesus.

The Authority of Jesus

In the middle of Luke's account of the Last Supper—just after the institution narrative—a dispute breaks out among the disciples about who among them is the greatest. Jesus responds:

> Earthly kings lord it over their people. Those who exercise authority over them are called their benefactors. Yet it cannot be that way with you. Let the greater among you be as the junior, the leader as the servant. Who, in fact, is the greater—he who reclines at table or he who serves the meal? Is it not the one who reclines at table? Yet I am in your midst as the one who serves you.
>
> Luke 22:25-27

[1] John L. McKenzie, *Authority in the Church* (New York: Sheed and Ward, 1966), p.85.

[2] See for example James Drane, *Authority and Institution* (Milwaukee: Bruce, 1966), pp. 13-32.

Jesus' response to the disciples (Luke refers to them a few verses earlier as "the apostles") sums up the way he understands his own life and at the same time provides an instruction on the way authority is to be exercised in his community. The passage obviously concerns those who are leaders in the community. They have authority, but Jesus is contrasting the way that they exercise it with the way authority is exercised "in the world." In the community of the disciples of Jesus, authority is expressed in service, the kind of service to others that Jesus embodied in his life and in the giving up of his life.

But a caution is in order here. Many things are attributed to Jesus in the gospels which reflect more the Easter faith and deeper understanding of the early Christian communities than the actual words and deeds of the historical Jesus. The gospels are not written transcriptions of his words and deeds, and therefore one cannot judge a gospel saying of Jesus to be authentic just because one or more of the evangelists attributes it to him. On the other hand, as Edward Schillebeeckx has pointed out, sayings or acts attributed to Jesus by the early community, while not necessarily spoken or performed by him, may be grounded in his inspiration and orientation.[3] Therefore in talking about whatever claims to authority might emerge from Jesus' preaching and activity, it is important not to assert more than historical critical biblical scholarship would recognize as being well grounded in Jesus himself.

Hans Küng has emphasized that the historical Jesus was not a priest, a theologian, a member of the ruling party, a social revolutionary, a monk or ascetic, a pious moralist, or a philosopher.[4] He did not belong to any of the established groups or parties within the Jewish community of his day which might have given him support. Jesus did not talk very much about himself. Yet the gospels frequently point out that, unlike the other teachers of his day, Jesus "taught with

[3]Edward Schillebeeckx, *Jesus* (New York: Crossroad, 1981), p. 98.

[4]Hans Küng, *On Being a Christian*, (Garden City, New York: Doubleday & Company, 1976), pp. 178-212.

authority" (Mk. 1:22; cf. Matt. 7:28-29; Lk. 4:32: Jn. 7:15 ff.).

Jesus' prophetic preaching was centered on God and on the approach of God's reign. He seems not to have identified himself with the Davidic messiah. On the basis of his life and teaching he has been most frequently described in the role of the eschatological prophet, the prophet of the end times, but one whose message differed from that of his predecessor John the Baptist. Where John's preaching warned of the coming judgment, Jesus' message was much more one of hope; he proclaimed the good news of God's graciousness and concern for all people.

Jesus' subject was the God he prayed to as Abba, not himself. Nevertheless, there is an unmistakable claim to authority implicit in what he said and did. First of all, though he did not attempt to abolish the Jewish Law, in his teaching he was not afraid to go beyond it (Matt. 5:22, 28, ff.). According to Walter Kasper, Jesus "placed his word, not against, but above, the highest authority in Judaism. And beyond the authority of Moses was the authority of God."[5] Schillebeeckx's position is more nuanced, but he points to a similar claim to authority in Jesus' attitude. He sees Jesus as radicalizing the Law by uncovering its deepest meaning. At the same time the praxis of the kingdom of God which he preached implied a critique of the Law as it was understood. Further, it implied even the possibility of going against what the Law specified.[6]

Second, Jesus proclaimed the forgiveness of sins, both in his parables (Matt. 18:23-35; Lk. 15:11-32) and also in deeds. The meals he shared with sinners and those considered outside the Law signified their participation in the reign of God (Matt. 11:19; Mk. 2:15-17; Lk. 15:2). The gospels remember not only the outrage expressed by the Pharisees and others over his practice of table fellowship (Matt. 11:19); they also indicate that those who heard Jesus recognized the deeper implications of his words and actions. Proclaiming the forgiveness of sins is a divine prerogative. When Jesus did so,

---

[5]Walter Kasper, *Jesus the Christ* (New York: Paulist Press, 1976), p. 102.

[6]Schillebeeckx, *Jesus*, p. 242.

they exclaimed, "He commits blasphemy" (Mk. 2:7).

Finally, through his preaching and call to discipleship Jesus presented his contemporaries with an eschatological choice. That choice is especially clear in a saying about the role of the Son of Man as judge which many scholars today regard as authentic: "I tell you, whoever acknowledges me before men—the Son of Man will acknowledge him before the angels of God. But the man who has disowned me in the presence of men will be disowned in the presence of the angels of God" (Lk. 12:8-9). There is an incredible claim to authority here, for Jesus is saying that those who reject him will be themselves rejected on the day of judgment; in other words, a decision for or against Jesus is the same thing as a decision for or against the reign of God.

Thus there is a clear claim to authority discernible in Jesus' preaching. In his person and work one encountered the reign of God. In stressing the importance of the encounter, Jesus gives evidence of the authority he possesses. Yet the claim to authority is more implicit than explicit. Jesus' approach to his own authority is self-effacing; he does not dwell on it or justify his authority to others (Mk. 11:27-33). While he makes demands of others, he never uses his authority to dominate them; he always leaves them free, to respond, or—like the rich young man—to go their own ways. When Jesus does speak of his own role, the gospels depict him as speaking in terms of service. This was the image he used to characterize his life; it also, apparently, provided for Jesus the key to understanding his own approaching death. Both Schillebeeckx and Kasper have shown how the notion of service is rooted in the Jesus of history and comes to expression specifically in relation to the question of how Jesus understood his death.

According to Kasper the kingdom of God that Jesus proclaimed received a personal embodiment in his life in the form of service. The service was not mere kindness, but one which brought about a healing of human alienation through "the remission of guilt towards God."[7] Everything Jesus did

[7]Kasper, *Jesus the Christ*, p. 120.

was determined by this kind of loving service. Against this background, Kasper argues, Jesus would have ultimately come to see the sacrifice of his life as also being a service for others. Thus he sees a number of disputed sayings connected with Jesus' death (Mk. 9:37) and with his death as a service for others (Mk. 10:45; 14:24) as having a historical basis in the life and intention of Jesus.[8]

Schillebeeckx's approach to the question of how Jesus understood his death is similar, but perhaps more radical. He focuses on a number of gospel texts dealing with Jesus as servant, all of them rooted, he argues, in what happened at the Last Supper. Mark 10:45 speaks of Jesus coming to serve and give his life in ransom for the many. Luke 22:27, a specific instruction on ministry, represents Jesus as saying at the Last Supper: "I am in your midst as the one who serves you." Luke 12:37b appears in a parousia parable which serves to link the earthly Jesus with the Jesus who will come on the last day. Schillebeeckx maintains that the verse, "I tell you, he will put on an apron, seat them at table, and proceed to wait on them," addressed to those servants whom the Master finds waiting, presupposes the tradition of the foot-washing. Finally, John 13:1-20 is the story of Jesus washing the feet of his disciples at the Last Supper.[9]

How do these texts reflect what happened at the Last Supper? The Last Supper accounts have been influenced by the liturgical traditions of the later church. But scholars are generally in agreement that at least the first half of Mark 14:25 (cf. Lk. 22:18) is authentic: "I solemnly assure you, I will never again drink of the fruit of the vine until the day when I drink it new in the reign of God." The second part of the sentence, starting with "until the day," according to Schillebeeckx is probably secondary. But the first part shows us how Jesus faced his death, with a confident assurance of salvation to his disciples.[10] Schillebeeckx writes:

[8]Ibid., pp. 120-121.
[9]Schillebeeckx, *Jesus*, pp. 303-305.
[10]Ibid., p. 309.

there is no getting around the historical fact that in the very face of death Jesus offers the cup of fellowship to his disciples; this is a token that he is not just passively allowing death to overcome him but has actively integrated in into his total mission, in other words, that he understands and is undergoing his death as a final and extreme service to the cause of God as the cause of men.[11]

Thus both Kasper and Schillebeeckx agree that Jesus understood his own life and death as a service. It is possible that his understanding of service derives from the figure of the Servant of Yahweh in Second Isaiah. Whether it did or not, there is considerable evidence that Jesus chose to take the role of a servant for the sake of the reign of God, and that this notion of himself as servant came to expression at the Last Supper. The authority that was implicit in his preaching took the form of service.

Conclusions

The inspiration and model for the exercise of any kind of authority in the church must be the example of Jesus himself. Not only did he understand his own vocation as service in the cause of God's reign, but he brought this understanding to expression at the Last Supper.

In the early Hellenist Jewish Christian churches this concept of service became a specifically ecclesial concept; that service in and for the Christian community we call today ministry. To express this the early Christians used the Greek word *diakonia* which in its original secular usage meant waiting at table. It was translated into Latin as *ministerium*. But its adaptation as a term for Christian ministry has its ultimate source in the Last Supper tradition and the subsequent elaboration of the theme of Jesus' death as an act of service which brings salvation.[12] Thus there is a liturgical

[11]Ibid., p. 311.

[12]See Schillebeeckx, *Jesus*, pp. 303-304; also J. Roloff, "Anfange der soteriologischen Deutung des Todes Jesu (Mk. 10:45 und Lk. 22:7)," *New Testament Studies* 19 (1972-3) 58-69.

connotation to this word, for the early Christians would have recognized the connection between their imitation of Jesus' loving service in the cause of God's reign and his table fellowship which was its expression and celebration.

3

Authority and Leadership
In Church History

In 1 Corinthians 12 Paul emphasizes that there is a variety of gifts (*charismata*) and ministries (*diakonia*) in the church. What is the source of these gifts and ministries? A charismatic approach to authority grounds all gifts and ministries in baptism. A hierarchical approach views the apostolic office, currently held by the bishops, as being of dominical institution, rooted in Jesus' choice of "the Twelve." However the separation between the pneumatological and the christological is not so easy to maintain. To gain some insight into this issue we need to review briefly the development of leadership and authority in the church.

Authority in the Early Christian Communities

While authority is present as a reality in the early Christian communities, the New Testament rarely uses the conventional expressions for office or authority in speaking of leaders in the church. Yves Congar has summarized the New Testament usage in this regard. *Taxis*, order, appears ten times, mostly in reference to the orders of Aaron and Melchizedek in the Jewish scriptures. *Timē*, in the sense of dignity or honor, appears only rarely; it is used of Jesus as the one placed over God's household (Hb. 3:3), and of his priesthood (Hb. 5:4). *Archē*, in the sense of power, is used three times in reference to civil power and nine times of the powers that Christ has or will overcome. It is never used of church authorities, nor does the word hierarchy ever appear. *Exousia*, which can mean both power and authority, appears ninety-three times in the New Testament, usually of the authority of God or Jesus; it is used three times of civil authorities. Seven times the term is used in an ecclesiological sense; five times it appears when Jesus gives his disciples authority to cast out demons (Matt. 10:1; Mk. 3:15; 6:7; Lk. 9:1; 10:19). Twice Paul uses the term in reference to the authority of an apostle for building up the community (2 Cor. 10:8; 13:10). Finally, *epitagē*, authority to command with the power to bind others, appears eight times in the Pauline literature (Rom. 16:26; 1 Cor. 7:25; 1 Tim. 1:1; Titus 1:3; 2:15). Paul is said to possess this authority (Titus 2:15) but he usually prefers not to use it (1 Cor. 7:6; 2 Cor. 8:8).[1]

There are of course various terms for those exercising leadership roles in the early Christian communities. In the first place are the apostles. Paul mentions rulers or leaders (*proistamenoi*: 1 Thes. 5:12; Rom. 12:8) apostles, prophets, teachers (1 Cor. 12:28); overseers and deacons (*episkopoi kai diakonoi*: Phil. 1:1), and ministers (*diakonos*: Rom. 16:1). He also refers to the hosts or heads of house churches (1 Cor. 16:19; Rom. 16:5; Philemon 2). The letter to the Ephesians refers to apostles, prophets, evangelists, pastors and teachers (Eph. 4:11). Leaders (*hēgoumenoi*) are mentioned (Hb. 13:7,17,24; Lk. 22:26). Prophets and teachers are still visible in later books (Acts 13:1; *Didache* 15:1) Matthew speaks of prophets and scribes (or wise men: Matt. 13:52; 23:34). Presbyters are frequently mentioned (James 5:14; Acts 11:30; 14:23; 20:17; 2 John 1; 3 John 1) or presbyter-bishops (1 and 2 Timothy, Titus; 1 Peter 5:1-4) and deacons (1 Tim. 3:8-13; *Didache* 15:1*).

But the basic concept, of which all of the terms are particular expressions, remains *diakonia*, service or ministry. As Paul makes clear, there is a diversity of ministries in the church just as there is a diversity of spiritual gifts or charisms (1 Cor. 12). Among them are various ministries of leadership,

---

[1]Yves Congar, *Power and Poverty in the Church* (Baltimore: Helicon, 1965), pp. 37-38.

a number of which eventually coalesced into an institutionalized office of pastoral authority or leadership. Who were these various leaders and what was the nature of their authority?

The Apostles. More traditional scholarship has tended to divide the New Testament period into the apostolic age and the sub-apostolic age. In the earlier period, the various communities were established and developed under the guidance of a group of missionaries and/or witnesses to the resurrection of Jesus, known from the earliest period as the apostles. But a number of difficulties must be faced in trying to define the concept of the apostle. The issue is complicated because there is no unified understanding of apostle in the New Testament.[2] Besides the role of the Twelve in the historical ministry of Jesus, both Paul and Luke-Acts present different conceptions of the apostle.

Paul's concept is developed largely on the basis of his own experience as a missionary; an apostle is one who has seen the risen Lord and has been sent forth to preach the Gospel. But another, broader and earlier concept of apostle can be recognized in Paul's writings; apostles are the early Christian missionaries (Rom. 16:7; 1 Thes. 2:7; 1 Cor. 9:5; 15:7). This view represents the original concept of an apostle, common among the early Christian communities. The exclusive identification of the Twelve as apostles is a later Lukan reflection. Luke recognizes the broader extension of the title apostle in the early church (Paul and Barnabas are called apostles in Acts 14:1-4); yet it is the Twelve, chosen by Jesus from within the wider circle of his disciples, which constitutes for him the paradigm of the apostle.

The historical existence of the Twelve is attested to by one of the earliest forms of the Easter kerygma (1 Cor. 15:5), though the later church no longer remembers all their names consistently. Even if they were not the only apostles in the primitive church, Raymond Brown states that "the majority

---

[2]For a survey of opinions on the meaning of "apostle" and bibliography see Rudolph Schnackenburg, "Apostolicity: the Present Position of Studies,"*One in Christ* 6 (1970) 243-73; also Francis H. Agnew, "The Origin of the NT Apostle-Concept: A Review of Research," *Journal of Biblical Literature* 105 (1986) 75-96.

of scholars still find persuasive the evidence that the twelve disciples of Jesus were considered apostles of the church from the beginning.[3]

In this traditional view the apostles, among whom the Twelve held pride of place, exercised roles of leadership in the primitive church. Edward Schillebeeckx acknowledges that the local church leaders were "ultimately under the over-sight of the apostles" and would refer to them when difficulties arose which they were unable to resolve.[4]

What was the source of their authority? Etymologically an apostle is one who has been "sent." Applying the word to an individual is virtually a unique New Testament usage, though recent research has returned to the view that the Christian understanding of apostle (as well as the rabbinic concept of the *saliah*) derives not from Christian experience but has its roots in the Jewish "sending convention" observable in the Old Testament.[5] The Twelve were chosen by Jesus during his historical ministry. Paul attributes his authority as an apostle to his experience of the risen Lord (Gal.1:1). The "apostles of the churches" (2 Cor. 8:23; cf. Phil. 2:25) were sent by early communities, sometimes for a specific task. Wayne Meeks describes their authority as derivative and limited.[6] But what is common to the various notions of apostle in the New Testament is this notion of the sending: "All from the community apostles to the apostles of Jesus Christ are commissioned agents sent to act in the name of others/another."[7]

Bengt Holmberg who analyzes authority in the primitive church from an historical and sociological point of view grounds the superior authority of the Jerusalem church and the original apostles on the basis of their closeness to "the *fons et origo* of all value and order in the Church—Jesus

[3]Raymond E. Brown, *Priest and Bishop: Biblical Reflections* (Paramus, New Jersey: Paulist Press, 1970), p. 49.

[4]Edward Schillebeeckx, *Ministry: Leadership in the Community of Jesus Christ* (New York: Crossroad, 1981), p.9.

[5]See Agnew, "The Origin of the NT Apostle-Concept" p. 91.

[6]Wayne A. Meeks, *The First Urban Christians: the Social World of the Apostle Paul* (New Haven: Yale University Press, 1983), p. 133.

[7]Ibid., p. 94.

Himself."[8] He maintains that this is a charismatic authority, since the primary type of authority in the primitive church is charismatic, but he also points out that the church itself should be characterized "as an institutionalized charismatic movement, since it exhibits elements of traditional and rational-legal authority."[9] Thus proximity to the person of Jesus and the ability to mediate his presence mean that the apostles and the prophets and teachers are the real authorities.[10]

Historical Leadership or Eschatological Symbol? Not all commentators today grant a unique leadership role to the apostles. Some use an egalitarian model to interpret the early Christian communities. According to Sandra Schneiders, the "divine choice of equality is the foundation and principle of unity among Jesus' disciples."[11] Elisabeth Schüssler Fiorenza describes the original Jesus movement as a "discipleship of equals," egalitarian in the sense that it was inclusive of women's leadership.[12]

Where the egalitarian model is used one generally finds the tendency to describe the role of the Twelve as eschatological, symbolizing the twelve tribes of the renewed Israel, rather than actual historical leadership. Schüssler Fiorenza takes this position, though she states that Luke seems to have historicized their function in regard to the mission to Israel.[13] Neither these functions nor that of eyewitness to the ministry and resurrection of Jesus is constitutive for church

---

[8]Bengt Holmberg, *Paul and Power: The Structure of Authority in the Primitive Church as Reflected in the Pauline Epistles* (Philadelphia: Fortress Press, 1980), p. 154.

[9]Ibid., p. 196.

[10]Ibid., pp. 195-197.

[11]Sandra M. Schneiders, "Evangelical Equality," *Spirituality Today* 38 (1986) 301.

[12]Elisabeth Schüssler Fiorenza, *In Memory of Her* (New York: Crossroad, 1983), p. 140.

[13]Elisabeth Schüssler Fiorenza, "The Twelve," in *Women Priests: A Catholic Commentary on the Vatican Declaration*, ed. Leonard Swidler and Arlene Swidler (New York: Paulist Press, 1977), pp. 117-120; see also Schuyler Brown, "Apostleship in the New Testament as an Historical and Theological Problem," *New Testament Studies* 30 (1984) 474-480.

ministry; her concern is to show that the lack of women among the Twelve does not mean that the contemporary church cannot ordain women to leadership roles. But in saying that the church "can entrust the apostolic ministry and power to whomever it chooses without maintaining any historical-lineal connection with the Twelve,"[14] she moves beyond the question of the ordination of women and implies that the Twelve have no necessary historical relation to the later ministry of the church.

What kind of role did the Twelve actually exercise? The New Testament does not provide a great deal of information. There is no evidence that they served as leaders of local churches or carried out a worldwide missionary effort. Most of them seem to have remained in Jerusalem.

But while the eschatological significance of the Twelve is important for the church, other commentators emphasize as well the important role they played as leaders in the early Christian community. Both Paul and Luke show the Jerusalem apostles involved in a decision that was decisive not just for the mission to Israel but for the future of the entire church, the decision concerning Gentile converts and the Mosaic Law. Luke's account of the apostolic "council" of Jerusalem in Acts 15 no doubt represents an idealized picture, but his emphasis on the role played by Peter is confirmed indirectly by Paul's own account of going up to Jerusalem for a "private conference with the leaders," to explain how he presented the Gospel to the Gentiles (Gal. 2:2). Paul's somewhat begrudging admission that he received the handclasp of fellowship from "the acknowledged pillars, James, Cephas, and John" (Gal. 2:9) testifies to the importance of the Jerusalem leadership, two of whom, John and Cephas (Peter), were members of the Twelve.

Bengt Holmberg acknowledges the "eschatological uniqueness" of the Jerusalem apostles, especially the Twelve. Precisely because they linked the community with the historical Jesus, he stresses that Paul felt he had to consult them and maintain fellowship with them.[15] He states that Gal. 2:1-10

[14]Schüssler Fiorenza, "The Twelve," p. 120.

[15]Holmberg, *Paul and Power*, p. 27.

leads to the conclusion that Paul and the Gentile mission of Antioch "is in fact dependent on what decision is taken by the Jerusalem authorities."[16] Raymond Brown summarizes the evidence as follows: "there is the image of a collective policy-making authority for the Twelve in the NT; and in the case of Peter ... the memory of pastoral responsibility. Otherwise the NT is remarkably vague about the kind of supervision exercised by members of the Twelve."[17]

Therefore there is some evidence that at least some of the Twelve were remembered as exercising an authoritative role in the earliest days of the Christian community. But this is not to suggest that they were involved in all important decisions or that the subsequent growth of the church took place entirely under their direction.

Leadership in the Early Communities. The apostles—the Twelve among them—were not the only leaders in the early church and therefore the only ones with authority. The church grew rapidly between 30 and 50 A.D. as a result of a great missionary effort. Elisabeth Schüssler Fiorenza has contributed to our knowledge of this period by recovering from the New Testament texts an earlier history which shows that in the Christian missionary movement women worked along with men as equal partners, founding and leading early churches.[18] This is still evident in Paul's letters, where women who played important roles are mentioned frequently. At the end of the letter to the Romans Paul commends to the community Phoebe, "*diakonos*" or minister of the church of Cenchreae (Rom. 16:9). He sends greetings to Prisca, along with her husband Aquila, his "fellow workers" and leaders of a house church in Rome (Rom. 16:3-5). And he calls Junia and her husband Andronicus "outstanding among the apostles" (Rom. 16:7). It is quite possible that

[16]Ibid., p. 28.

[17]Raymond E. Brown, "*Episkope* and *Episkopos*: The New Testament Evidence," *Theological Studies* 41 (1980) 325.

[18]Schüssler Fiorenza, *In Memory of Her*, pp. 160 ff.

many of the early missionaries were partners, husbands and wives working together.[19]

Schillebeeckx also stresses the openness to the ministry of both men and women in the early Hellenist-Jewish communities. He argues that Paul came to know an egalitarian view of the church from the early tradition: "Every member of the community had *de facto* authority in the community on the basis of his or her own inspiration by the Spirit."[20] This pneumatic ecclesiology did not exclude leadership or authority, but "authority must be one filled with the Spirit, from which no Christian, man or woman, is excluded in principle on the basis of the baptism of the Spirit."[21] Paul asked that the community leaders at Thessalonica be shown special respect (1 Thes. 5:12), a fact which for Schillebeeckx indicates at least a latent opposition towards what some apparently perceived as "non-egalitarian attitudes" in an originally egalitarian church.[22]

In Paul's letters one can see the rich variety of gifts and ministries in some of the early missionary churches. In the list of charisms in 1 Corinthians 12:28 Paul names "first apostles, second prophets, third teachers, then miracle workers, healers, assistants, administrators, and those who speak in tongues." In Romans 12:6-8 he lists the charisms of prophecy, ministry, the teacher, the exhorter, the alms giver, the ruler or leader, and the one who does works of mercy. He also mentions marriage and celibacy as charisms (1 Cor. 7:7).

It is difficult to speak of *office* in Paul's churches. By office is understood a position of authority received through appointment to exercise a permanent public ministry within the community. This is usually termed an "institutional

[19]Ibid., p. 169; see Schüssler Fiorenza's comments on the tendency of later interpreters to eliminate the women's names from the text by understanding Junia as short for the male Junianus and by translating *diakonos* in the case of Phoebe as deaconess; p. 47.

[20]Edward Schillebeeckx, *The Church with a Human Face*, (New York: Crossroad, 1985), p. 37.

[21]Ibid., p. 39.

[22]Ibid., p. 60.

ministry," in contrast to a "charismatic ministry," arising spontaneously to address immediate needs in a community through the Holy Spirit. Paul uses the term *charism* to refer to those various gifts or manifestations of the Spirit which enable a person to perform some service for the common good of the community (1 Cor. 12:7).[23] The roles of leadership recognizable among the charism have not yet been "institutionalized," for Paul does not mention any ritual or sign of appointment to what would then be called an office. In this period the ministerial vocabulary tends to be rather functional and fluid.

But it would be inaccurate to conclude that the theology of the various charisms that Paul develops was actually the structuring principle of the Pauline churches, particularly the church of Corinth. As Holmberg emphasizes, in 1 Corinthians 12-14, Paul was not describing the Corinthian church but attempting to transform it: "The primary problem was the Corinthian overestimation of glossolalia (*ta pneumatika*), and the concomitant belief that some Christians had a special endowment of Spirit, manifesting itself 'pneumatically'."[24]

Some of the charisms named indicate more permanent leadership roles. The prophets and teachers named after the apostles are usually recognized as local community leaders. Schillebeeckx calls them "incipient local leaders and pioneers."[25] Wayne Meeks points to the few roles common to all the lists, to Paul's ranking of apostles, prophets, and teachers in 1 Cor. 12:28, and to the evidence that some leaders were supported by the congregations from a very early period (Gal. 6:6) as evidence "that some degree of formalization had already taken place."[26] In proposing a tripartite classification of the modes of authority present in the local communities Meeks recognizes the balance between the more dramatic "pneumatic" gifts and those roles which

---

[23]For a good discussion of the relation of office to charism see Carolyn Osiek, "Relation of Charism to Rights and Duties in the New Testament Church," *The Jurist* 41 (1981) 295-313.

[24]Bengt Holmberg, *Paul and Power*, p. 120; cf. pp. 201-203.

[25]Schillebeeckx, *Church With a Human Face*, p. 79.

[26]Meeks, *The First Urban Christians*, p. 135.

would later be associated with office; he points to "visible manifestations of Spirit-possession, position, and association with apostles and other supralocal persons of authority."[27] All of these could be considered as charisms.

The Emergence of a Pastoral Office. As the original witnesses and missionary founders passed from the scene and the church moved into its second and third generations, an institutionalized office of leadership began to emerge.[28] A number of New Testament books contain material which reflect questions from this period about leadership and authority. Matthew recognizes the authority of local church leaders to a considerable degree but seems concerned about a type of "nascent clericalism" which is evident in his warnings against "ostentatious religious clothing and paraphernalia . . . the desire for first seats at the religious meetings . . . and the desire to be addressed with special titles" (Matt. 23:5-10).[29] The dispute among the disciples over rank in the synoptics (Mk. 10:35-45; Matt. 20:20-28; Lk. 22:24-27) is also concerned with authority. Form criticism recognizes this as a tradition on ministry and church order rooted in a saying of Jesus about his own role of humble service which was adapted by the early communities as an instruction on the exercise of authority in the church. A variant tradition in 1 Peter 5:1-4 instructs the presbyters (literally elders) to exercise their authority without "lording it over" others.[30]

Increasingly the presbyter/bishops (the two terms were not at first clearly distinguished) took over the roles exercised in earlier times by the prophets, teachers, and leaders (*proistamenoi*) and probably by the leaders of the house churches. Their responsibility frequently included both community leadership and teaching. The expression "pastors and

---

[27]Ibid., p. 136.

[28]See Thomas P. Rausch, *The Roots of the Catholic Tradition* (Wilmington, Delaware: Michael Glazier, 1986), pp. 131-139.

[29]John P. Meier in Raymond E. Brown and John P. Meier, *Antioch and Rome* (New York: Paulist Press, 1983), p. 70.

[30]See John Hall Elliott, "Ministry and Church Order in the NT: A Traditio-Historical Analysis (1 Pt 5, 1-5 & plls)," *The Catholic Biblical Quarterly* 32 (1970) 367-391.

teachers," introduced by a single article in Ephesians 4:11, indicates an office of pastoral leadership which included both functions. The same dual responsibility is attributed in Acts (20:17-35) and the Pastoral Epistles to the presbyter-bishops who must watch over preaching and teaching. These local leaders were frequently portrayed as succeeding to the pastoral care of the apostles for the churches, both in terms of guarding the apostolic tradition (Acts 20:29-31; 2 Tim. 1:14; 2:2) and by various efforts to link their ministry with that of the apostles themselves (1 Pet. 5:1; Acts 14:23; 1 Tim. 5:22; Titus 1:5). The laying on of hands, a practice borrowed from Judaism, emerged in this same period as the sign of appointment to office.

Raymond Brown notes that "in churches associated with the three great apostolic figures of the NT, Paul, James, and Peter, presbyters were known and established in the last third of the century."[31] The threefold ministry of a local bishop, assisted by presbyters and deacons, is in place at Antioch and probably in a number of other churches shortly after the end of the New Testament period. Ignatius of Antioch about 112 A.D. provided for it a theological justification: the bishop represents God, the presbyters take the place of the apostles, while the deacons represent Christ (Magn. 6.1; Trall. 3.1).

By the end of the second century the threefold ministry was in place throughout the church. Each local church was presided over by a bishop, assisted by a college of presbyters and the deacons. The struggle against montanism and gnosticism served to strengthen the bishops' authority. Montanus and his disciples Prisca and Maximilla were ecstatic prophets who claimed that their utterances represented a direct revelation. This stressed the special authority of the spiritually gifted. Against this, the conviction developed that the deposit of revelation had been closed with the passing of the apostles. Similarly, to counter the gnostics' claim of secret, unwritten tradition going back to Jesus, appeal was made to the true apostolic tradition publicly

[31] Raymond E. Brown, "*Episkope* and *Episkopos*," p. 336.

proclaimed and handed on through the churches with apostolic foundation. Writers such as Hegesippus, Irenaeus, and Tertullian used the lists of the bishops of these churches to demonstrate their visible continuity with the apostolic period and in this way the authenticity of their doctrinal tradition. For problems affecting a number of churches the bishops of an area met together in council even before Nicaea (325). Thus from the second century the bishops were recognized as successors of the apostles, both as leaders of the local churches and as teachers who could authoritatively interpret the apostolic tradition.

The threefold ministry was to prove remarkably effective in providing for pastoral care and leadership at the local level while at the same time developing a structure through the office of the bishop for linking the various churches together into a universal communion. But its emergence was not without some loss.

One such loss was the Pauline concept of the multiplicity of charisms. In the later New Testament books the term charism was restricted to the ministry of church leaders (1 Pet. 4:10), to those who receive the laying on of hands (1 Tim. 4:14; 2 Tim. 1:6).

Also lost was the openness to the ministry of women which can be discerned in the earliest communities. The later New Testament books contain a number of injunctions and traditions which had the effect of placing women in a position of subordination. From Greco-Roman sources came various household codes which emphasized a patriarchal domestic order based on the submission of wives to husbands, children to parents, and slaves to masters (Col. 3:18-4:1; Eph. 5:22-6:9; 1 Pet. 2:13-3:7; Titus 2:5-9). A similar instruction in 1 Timothy contains an injunction against women teaching; its presence implies that there were women who were teaching in the community (1 Tim. 2:12).

Resistance to the Pastoral Office. Not all the communities, however, welcomed the institutionalized office. Some tried to resist this development, apparently preferring the more fluid structuring of an earlier generation.

One example of this is provided by the church at Corinth.

About the year 96 A.D. a letter known as 1 Clement was sent from the church of Rome to the church at Corinth because of a schism that was developing there. Some agitators in the community had inspired a revolt against the local presbyters which had led to their removal, without cause, from their office (44:6; 47:6). It is interesting to note that this church, which has become for some the paradigm of the charismatically structured community, had problems with unity in the time of Paul and was still having them some forty years later. The author of 1 Clement admonishes the Corinthians to respect their duly elected leaders. In the process he urges them to recognize that the church order now in place there had been established by the apostles and reflects the divine plan, and thus he establishes the formal principle of apostolic succession (42:1-4). The church at Corinth accepted Rome's intervention; around the year 170 Dionysius, bishop of Corinth, writes to Soter, bishop of Rome, that the letter of Clement is still being read in the liturgical assembly (Eusebius, *History* 4.23.11).

The Johannine community provides another interesting example of a gradual acceptance of an institutionalized office of ministry. This community may come the closest to being an egalitarian discipleship. Eduard Schweizer says that in the Johannine ecclesiology "there is no longer any kind of special ministry, but only the direct union with God through the Spirit who comes to every individual; here there are neither offices nor even different charismata" (cf. 1 John 2:20, 27).[32]

Raymond Brown does not go as far as Schweizer. In his study of the Johannine community he argues that Schweizer assumes more in regard to ecclesiastical ministry than is actually known; furthermore, there are "contrary indications" in the Johannine epistles.[33] But Brown describes the Johannine Christians as a community apart, distinguished by their high christology and their apparent lack of interest

[32]Eduard Schweizer, *Church Order in the New Testament* (London: SCM, 1961), p. 127.

[33]Raymond E. Brown, *The Community of the Beloved Disciple,* (New York: Paulist Press, 1979), p. 87.

in developing church structures at the very time that other Christian communities were stressing them. In the fourth gospel one does not find an emphasis on teaching authority or the apostolic tradition, the technical term "apostle" does not appear, and there are no words of Jesus instituting the sacraments of baptism or the Eucharist as one finds in Matthew 28:19 and Luke 22:19. The Beloved Disciple is portrayed as closer to Jesus than Peter. The community itself is a community of disciples guided by the Spirit; what is stressed is the teaching role of the Paraclete who will maintain the community in all truth (John 16:13).[34]

Most interesting for our considerations here is the point Brown makes about the subsequent history of the Johannine community. He sees in the Johannine epistles, written around the year A.D. 100, the beginning of a schism which was to split the community and lead part of it ultimately into gnosticism. Both theological and ecclesiological factors contributed to the breakup. Theologically, the secessionists so emphasized the divinity of Jesus that their christology became docetic, unable to comprehend the salvific importance of Jesus' humanity, and correspondingly, the importance of ethical behavior in the lives of the members of the community. At the same time, their realized eschatology and a pneumatology which could appeal, not to authority but only to the inner experience of each believer, left the community ecclesiologically helpless when differences polarized the community into two sides, with the members of each claiming to be in possession of the Spirit.[35]

The result was the breakup of the community. Those Johannine Christians associated with the author of the Johannine epistles learned from their experience, Brown argues, and came to accept the authoritative teaching office of the presbyter-bishops which was becoming widespread in the other churches. He suggests that the final chapter of the fourth gospel, with its emphasis on the pastoral role of Peter

[34]Ibid., pp. 86-88; Brown discusses the Johannine ecclesiology at greater length in his *The Churches the Apostles Left Behind* (New York: Paulist Press, 1984), pp. 84-104.

[35]Brown, *Community*, pp. 110-144.

(John 21:15-17) was added to convince the Johannine Christians that the pastoral authority exercised in the other churches was instituted by Jesus himself.[36] But the secessionists—perhaps the larger part of the community—continued moving towards docetism and gnosticism. They brought elements of Johannine theology to these emerging second century movements but were themselves lost to Christian history.

Gnosticism presents a third interesting case for the study of emerging structures of authority. In her study of the Nag Hammadi texts Elaine Pagels maintains that gnostics were among those who opposed the developing church hierarchy.[37] At least some gnostic groups rejected in principle any distinctions within the community based on office or function, including that of clergy and laity.

One of the most influential forms of the gnostic movement was that inspired by Valentinus, who founded a sect in Rome in the second century.[38] According to Pagels, Valentinian gnosticism taught its initiates to reject all ecclesiastical authority on the basis of its deriving, not from the supreme and utterly transcendent God, but from the "creator" (*demiurgos*), a lesser divine being.[39] These Valentinian gnostics were egalitarian. Irenaeus describes a group of them in Lyons, the followers of Marcus who claimed that each initiated member was directly inspired by the Spirit (Adv. Haer. 1.13.3). At their meetings or "feasts" they drew lots to determine who would prophesy (1.13.4). In Pagels' interpretation of the text, the traditional ecclesiastical functions were doled out to those present: "Whoever received a certain lot apparently was designated to take the role of *priest*; another was to offer the sacrament, as *bishop*; another would read the Scriptures for worship, and others would address the

---

[36]Ibid., pp. 159-162

[37]Elaine Pagels, *The Gnostic Gospels* (New York: Random House, 1979), p. 40.

[38]For a general introduction to Valentinus and his followers see Bentley Layton, *The Gnostic Scriptures* (Garden city, New York: Doubleday, 1987), pp. 217-222; 267-275.

[39]Pagels, *The Gnostic Gospels*, pp. 32-39.

group as a *prophet*, offering extemporaneous spiritual instructions."[40]

Pagels' interpretation may be going beyond what the text allows, but Tertullian in his "Prescription Against the Heretics" describes something similar. He criticizes a heretical group as being "without authority, without discipline," for among them "it is doubtful who is a catechumen, and who a believer," while their women "are bold enough to teach, to dispute, to enact exorcisms, to undertake cures—it may be even to baptize" (41). Furthermore, in allowing everyone to do everything, they overturned the traditional ecclesiastical order:

> Their ordinations are carelessly administered, capricious, changeable. At one time they put *novices* in office; at another time, men who are bound to some secular employment. . . . Nowhere is promotion easier than in the camp of rebels, where the mere fact of being there is a foremost service. And so it comes to pass that to-day one man is their bishop, to-morrow another; to-day he is a deacon who to-morrow is a reader; to-day he is a presbyter who to-morrow is a layman. For even on laymen do they impose the functions of priesthood (41).[41]

Pagels is correct in recognizing an egalitarian (and feminist) dimension to some parts of the movement. She describes the gnostics as elitists who stressed a higher level of understanding and the quality of their personal relationships and she contrasts them with the more inclusive orthodox Christians, among whom membership was determined by objective criteria such as creeds, ritual, and a strong emphasis on episcopal authority.[42] But her suggestion that both the gnostics and those she calls the orthodox Christians were legitimate expressions of primitive Christianity is highly problematic. Gnosticism was an aberrant phenomenon which

[40]Ibid., p. 41.

[41] *The Ante-Nicene Fathers,* Vol. III, ed. Alexander Roberts and James Donaldson (Grand Rapids, Michigan: Wm. Eerdmans, 1978), p. 263.

[42]Pagels, *The Gnostic Gospels,* pp. 102-106.

emerged in the mid-second century, often combining philosophical speculations and mythological elements with concepts and images borrowed from Christianity, particularly from the Johannine literature, as we saw above. The gnostic movement could not sustain itself. Never really unified as a system of thought and without adequate provision for leadership, the movement remained splintered and soon disappeared from Christian history.

Presiding at the Eucharist. The New Testament does not provide much information about who presided at the Eucharist. From parallels with Jewish practice, it is possible but not certain that the householders or heads of the house churches led the communities that gathered in their homes and presided at their Eucharists. There is some evidence that the prophets and teachers included eucharistic presidency among their roles. Acts 13:2 shows the prophets and teachers at Antioch "engaged in the liturgy (*leitourgountōn*) of the Lord." The *Didache* recognizes that the prophets could improvise when leading the Eucharist (10.7); it also urges the community to elect bishops and deacons with the encouragement that "they too conduct (*leitourgousi*) the liturgy of the prophets and teachers (15.1).

When the laying on of hands emerged as the ritual sign of appointment to office, it was a sign of appointment to the ministry of community leadership, not to a particular function. The first clear attempt to link the Eucharist with church leaders appears in Ignatius of Antioch: "You should regard that Eucharist as valid which is celebrated either by the bishop or by someone he authorizes" (Smyrneans 8.1).[43] But what is becoming increasingly clear today is that in the early tradition eucharistic presidency was linked to those who presided over the community; the role was not seen as explicitly

---

[43] John H. Elliott suggests that Luke's placing the dispute among the disciples over rank in the context of the institution of the Eucharist (Lk. 22:24-27) may represent one of the "early stages of a trend associating ministry and Eucharist which later becomes the basis upon which the post-apostolic church builds"; "Ministry and Church Order in the NT," p. 385.

sacerdotal until the early third century.[44] For a person to be installed into the episcopal or presbyteral office the election, or at least approval, by the community was necessary.[45] Schillebeeckx has placed great stress on canon 6 of the Council of Chalcedon (451) which decreed that an ordination without assignment to a particular community was invalid.[46]

The Clericalization of the Pastoral Office.

Important as the bishops were, particularly in the area of doctrine, they were not the only ones recognized as having authority. Teachers such as Justin Martyr, Tertullian, Clement of Alexandria, and Origen, though not bishops, had considerable authority. The martyrs possessed authority; so did the confessors, those who had been imprisoned and suffered for the sake of Christ. According to the *Apostolic Tradition* of Hippolytus (9), a confessor could be considered a presbyter, though if he were to be selected as bishop, he would have to receive the laying on of hands. As the ascetic or monastic movement spread in the third and fourth centuries, others were recognized as having authority on the basis of holiness of life. The practice of appointing monks bishops was one way of trying to deal with the rivalry which sometimes developed between the ascetics and those who exercised the church's pastoral office, the clergy.[47]

If the clergy, particularly the bishops, were the ordinary authorities, in the second and third centuries they were not yet distinguished from the community, either by dress or by special privileges. Certainly the New Testament does not distinguish between "clergy" and "laity." As Yves Congar has written, the tension in the church of the martyrs was

[44]Hervé-Marie Legrand, "The Presidency of the Eucharist According to the Ancient Tradition," *Worship* 53 (1979) 427.

[45]See David N. Power, "The Basis for Official Ministry in the Church," *The Jurist* 41 (1981) 320-321.

[46]Schillebeeckx, *Ministry*, pp. 38-48.

[47]Cf. Robert B. Eno, *Teaching Authority in the Early Church* (Wilmington, Delaware: Michael Glazier, 1984), p. 19.

between the church and the world, not between the various categories of Christians themselves.[48] But that situation was to change considerably.

Perhaps more important than anything else in this regard was the transition the church went through in the fourth century from a countercultural church persecuted by the Empire to an established church. With Constantine's Edict of Milan in 313 the church received legal status and its officials began to receive an official place in the Roman empire.[49] The church could own land and began to acquire buildings. Like the pagan priests, bishops and presbyters were exempted from taxes and civil duties. Bishops began to receive certain honors and privileges. In the fifth century they began to wear the insignia of high officials such as the *pallium* and the stole. Before long other clergy were wearing distinctive clothing. At the same time the liturgy was becoming more ornate, incorporating processions, rich vestments, gold vessels and furnishings, incense, and ceremonies borrowed from the imperial court.

An increasing emphasis on the cultic aspect of the ordained minister's role also contributed to a growing tension between laity and clergy, with a consequent accumulation of privileges for the latter. Edward Schillebeeckx has emphasized a number of factors which contributed to this clericalization of the ordained ministry. One was the growth of the church in the third and fourth centuries which led to the emergence of the "country priest," really the first of what we today call parish priests. These were pastors who served rural communities. Since one of their primary functions was to preside at the local liturgies, they became "Mass priests." Thus their roles were different from those of the presbyters in the large urban churches who assisted the bishop as members of his presbyteral council and "concelebrated" with him at the Eucharist. One consequence of this development was an increasing emphasis on the relationship between the priest and

[48]Yves Congar, "The Historical Development of Authority," in *Problems of Authority*, ed. John M. Todd (Baltimore: Helicon Press, 1962), p. 135.

[49]See Congar, *Power and Poverty in the Church* (Baltimore: Helicon, 1965), pp. 111-131; also Schillebeeckx, *Church with a Human Face*, pp. 141-153.

the Eucharist, rather than on the relationship between the Eucharist and the community.[50]

Another factor was the practice of private celebrations of the Eucharist which Schillebeeckx maintains began early in the sixth century in connection with the veneration of relics.[51] This had the effect of weakening considerably the link between ordained ministry and community itself. The priest was becoming a sacred person whose identity was defined in terms of a cultic function. A third factor was the law of abstinence from sexual intercourse for married priests prior to celebrating the Eucharist, and ultimately, clerical celibacy.[52]

The Germanic influence making itself felt in the Empire around the time of Charlemagne (d. 814) also contributed to the growth of clerical and episcopal privileges. Congar calls attention to the importance placed on gestures of handing over and touching significant objects, pledging obedience by placing one's hands between the hands of a superior, handing over instruments or insignia to incorporate one into an office. The crozier or pastoral staff appeared in Spain in the seventh century and in Gaul in the eighth. About this same time the episcopal ring appeared in both regions. From Byzantium was borrowed the practice of genuflecting and the kissing of the feet.[53] These practices enriched the liturgy, but they also contributed to a growing emphasis on priestly and episcopal power.

Similarly, the papacy inherited the insignia of the Roman empire. The popes began to wear the diadem or crown, the phrygium or round, white mitre, the red tunic, and to carry the scepter. Gregory VII (1073-1085) claimed exclusive right to wear imperial insignia in his *Dictatus Papae*. While the papacy took on the representations, images, and titles of a monarch based on the imperial model, the church itself became inculturated in a highly hierarchical feudal system

---

[50]Schillebeeckx, *Church with a Human Face*, pp. 140-143.

[51]Ibid., pp. 159-160.

[52]Ibid., p. 153.

[53]Congar, *Power and Poverty*, p. 118.

which it reflected in its ranks of officials, insignia, titles, different lifestyles and forms of dress. Papal absolutism reached its high point under Boniface VIII (1294-1303) who claimed in his famous bull *Unam Sanctam* "that it is absolutely necessary for the salvation of all men that they submit to the Roman pontiff" (DS 875). Boniface introduced the triple-crowned tiara; Congar points out that this tiara, which rises from a wide base to a single point at the top "was an apt expression of the idea of pontifical monarchy and a quasi-pyramidal concept of the Church."[54] The Conciliarist movement, which in the fourteenth century grew out of the struggle to resolve the dilemma caused by the "western schism" with its rival claimants to the papal throne, was in part a reaction to papal absolutism and the abuse of power.

Bishops and Theologians

In the Middle Ages the work of the canonists and the growing prestige of the university *doctores* led to the emergence of a new kind of authority which was based on scholarship. The canonists of the twelfth and thirteenth centuries developed a nuanced ecclesiology which held that the ultimate criteria for determining the validity of an ecclesiastical pronouncement or teaching were to be found, not in its source (whether pope or council) and juridical authority, but rather in the intrinsic truth of the decision and in its reception by the church.[55] And Congar has shown that the authority of the professors of theology in the great medieval universities, particularly that of Paris, was associated with that of the church fathers and for a time assumed "a debatable primacy."[56]

The university theologians (who were of course clerics)

---

[54]Ibid., pp. 125-126.

[55]See Brian Tierney, "Only the Truth Has Authority': The Problem of 'Reception' in the Decretists and in Johannes de Turrecremata," in *Law, Church, and Society: Essays in Honor of Stephan Kuttner*, ed. Kenneth Pennington and Robert Somerville (University of Pennsylvania Press, 1977), pp. 69-96.

[56]Yves Congar, "Theologians and the Magisterium in the West: From the Gregorian Reform to the Council of Trent," *Chicago Studies* 17 (1978) 214.

collaborated with the hierarchy by serving on commissions to evaluate theological positions, condemning those whose opinions were considered heterodox, even preparing papal censures. In this way they played a considerable role in judging what was to be considered orthodox. Avery Dulles points out that the "doctrinal decrees of several general councils (Lyons I, 1245; Lyons II, 1274; and Vienne, 1312) were submitted to universities for approval before being published."[57] The university theologians also advanced theology by their own work, though cautiously, lest they themselves incure papal condemnation.

Thus the place of these theologians was clearly recognized. Thomas Aquinas distinguished between two types of *magisterium* or teaching, that of the bishops and that of the doctors. The word magisterium comes from the Latin *magister*, master, which connoted someone with authority but was used particularly of teachers. The bishops with their supervisory responsibility held the "magisterium of the pastoral chair" (*magisterium cathedrae pastoralis*); the theologians, whose competence was based on learning, held the "magisterium of the professor's chair" (*magisterium cathedrae magistralis*).[58] Congar points out that the word magisterium took on its present meaning (i.e., that of the teaching office exercised by the pope and bishops) only under Gregory XVI, about 1830.[59] There are precedents for the participation of church representatives other than bishops in ecumenical councils. At Lateran Council IV (1215) besides the 400 bishops, 800 abbots and priors participated, while at the Council of Florence (1437-42), a council which sought to reunite the Eastern and Western churches, the Latin side voted in three estates: bishops, abbots and religious, and the lower clergy.[60]

[57]Avery Dulles, *A Church to Believe In* (New York: Crossroad, 1982), p. 109.

[58]Yves Congar, "A Semantic History of the Term 'Magisterium'," in *Readings in Moral Theology No. 3, The Magisterium and the Theologian,* ed. Charles E. Curran and Richard A. McCormick (New York: Paulist Press, 1982), p. 303; (cf. Quodl. III 9 ad 3).

[59]Congar, "Theologians and the Magisterium," p. 210.

[60]See Ladislas Orsy, "Some Questions from History," *America* 158 (1988) 300.

The authority of the doctors or professors continued to grow until it began to come into conflict with that of the bishops. According to Francis Sullivan, the university faculties of theology dominated the Councils of Constance (1415) and Basel (1439): "Anyone with a doctorate in theology or canon law was given full voting rights, with the astonishing result that at the thirty-fourth session of the Council of Basel (25 June 1439) there were three hundred *doctores* with voting rights, and only seven bishops. This, of course, was an aberration, and the council ended in a fiasco."[61]

Basel and its predecessor, the Council of Constance, gave expression to the conciliarist theory popular in the fourteenth and fifteenth centuries. The central issue was that of authority in the church, and how it was to be exercised. "The question raised by the Council of Constance was whether the authority of the universal church resided in a general council made up of bishops, abbots, doctors of theology and canon lawyers, conceived of as a kind of ecclesiastical parliament, distinct from and ultimately superior to the executive, the pope."[62] Constance attempted to answer this question affirmatively in the decree *Haec Sancta* which espoused the conciliarist teaching, but the church did not receive this decree. The Council of Florence (1438-1445) emphasized papal authority, clearly a reaction to the excesses of Basel. Since that council the Roman Catholic Church has understood a general council as exercising the authority of the universal church when the assembled bishops act both with and under the pope.

But even after Florence theologians continued to play an important role in judging orthodoxy; as Congar and Sullivan note, it was scholastic theologians who examined and developed the critique of Luther's forty-one theses which led to their condemnation in the bull *Exsurge Domine* (June 15, 1520).[63] At the Council of Trent theologians served on some

[61]Francis A. Sullivan, *Magisterium: Teaching Authority in the Church* (Mahwah, New Jersey: Paulist Press, 1983), p. 182.

[62]Ibid., p. 89.

[63]Congar, "Theologians and the Magisterium," p. 217; Sullivan, *Magisterium*, p. 182.

of the congregations of bishops and were called upon to speak at the plenary sessions.

In the period from Trent to Vatican II authority in the Roman Catholic Church became ever more clerically understood and more centralized in the papal office. Vatican I, with its definition of papal primacy and infallibility, represents the dogmatic high water mark. But even during this period, there was provision to include some who did not hold the episcopal office in the church's councils. Avery Dulles has pointed out that cardinals, abbots, and general superiors of religious orders took part as voting members at Trent, Vatican I, and Vatican II.[64] Therefore even though it is true that the Roman Catholic Church recognizes the order of bishops as the successors to the apostles in teaching authority,[65] there is historical precedent for finding ways for others with theological, ministerial, or professional competence to have some part in the exercise of the church's magisterium. With Vatican II a monarchical understanding of authority began to give way to a more collegial one. But the renewal of structures and life which it began has not yet been fully implemented.

Conclusions

At the end of this brief and admittedly selective review of the nature and history of authority in the church it is time to draw some conclusions

1. In the earliest days of the community the Jerusalem apostles, with at least some of the Twelve among them, were recognized as leaders because of their proximity to Jesus. Paul and Barnabas as representatives of the Gentile mission of Antioch acknowledged their authority and in turn were recognized by the Jerusalem leaders. The obvious evidence of Peter's authority in the earliest days should make one

[64]Dulles, *A Church to Believe In*, p. 111.

[65]LG no. 22, in *The Documents of Vatican II*, ed. Walter M. Abbott (New York: America Press, 1966), p. 43.

cautious about suggesting that the eschatological role of the Twelve did not include actual, historical leadership. Their authority is not merely grounded in the Spirit but has historical roots in their call and missioning by the historical Jesus; that is to say, it is not just pneumatological, but also christological in its foundation.

2. Recent scholarship has recovered the important roles played by women in the early missionary movements. It is evident both that women were active in founding churches and exercising leadership ministries in them in the earliest period and that the later New Testament books reflect a hardening of the communities against women in leadership roles. The openness of the church to the ministry of women in primitive Christianity has implications for the church of today and tomorrow.

3. Just as the New Testament recognizes the diversity of charisms it also recognizes a church office which it portrays as linked to the ministry of the apostles. The apostles did associate others with them in their ministry. On the other hand a structured office of pastoral leadership developed slowly and not always simultaneously in the different communities. Some resisted it, but those which did not incorporate it lost communion with the other churches and lapsed into heterodoxy, ultimately to disappear from Christian history.

The problem is not office but the loss of the other charisms. It belongs to the office of church leadership to regulate the charisms and to provide for their expression. The ordained minister presides over the community, uniting it around the eucharistic table and expressing its unity with the worldwide church catholic and with the church of the apostles. An egalitarian ecclesiology which would exclude in principle the reality of an office within the church is both sociologically naive and unhistorical. What is important is to provide for equality of opportunity and to recover a proper and equitable balance between charism and office. Vatican II, with its emphasis on what it calls "various gifts, both hierarchical and charismatic," is a step in the right direction.[66]

4. The relation between office and charism is best described as dialectical,[67] rather than one of domination and subordination. Office is rooted in charism; an office bestowed without a discerned charism may be valid but it is ineffective. Charisms challenge office and institution, but unregulated, they can become divisive, even chaotic. Institutional authority may seem to have the last word, but in the final analysis the decisions and teachings of authority must find reception by the whole church, as we will consider later.

5. Eucharistic presidency belongs to the function of presiding over the community. The traditional language of priesthood (*hiereus/sacerdos*) for the church leader has served to underline the nature of the church as a eucharistic community, but it has also contributed to a onesided concept of a primarily cultic ordained ministry. In the light of the original nexus between leading the community and eucharistic presidency, Leonardo Boff's suggestion that lay community coordinators be authorized to preside at the Eucharist for communities lacking ordained ministers may not be so untraditional.[68] Some Protestant traditions permit this, though usually under carefully specified conditions.[69] Certainly the contemporary Roman Catholic problem of local churches not being able to celebrate the Eucharist would not have arisen in the early church, for a community would always choose a local leader as presider who could then be

[66]LG no. 4; cf. nos. 7,12; Carolyn Osiek presents at greater length the teaching of Vatican II on the charisms; "Relation of Charism to Rights and Duties," p. 295; at the same time she critiques the Council's operative assumption "that the spiritual gifts or charisms given to the People of God do not include ministry, which belongs only to those in sacred orders" p. 296.

[67]See Holmberg's discussion of the dialectical nature of authority in the primitive church in *Paul and Power*, pp. 198-201; also Dulles' theses on the relation between institution and charism in his *A Church to Believe In*, pp. 29-40.

[68]Leonardo Boff, *Ecclesiogenesis: The Base Communities Reinvent the Church* (Maryknoll, New York: Orbis Books, 1986), pp. 61-75.

[69]See Gaston Westphal, "Role and Limit of Pastoral Delegation to Laymen for the Celebration of the Eucharist in the Protestant Reformed Churches," in *Roles in the Liturgical Assembly*, trans. Matthew J. O'Connell (New York: Pueblo, 1977), pp. 275-290.

appointed with the help of the heads of neighboring churches.[70]

6. Since the second and third centuries the bishops have been recognized as authentic teachers whose interpretation of the apostolic tradition was considered normative. For Roman Catholicism the papal-episcopal magisterium is the church's teaching authority. But without taking anything away from the authority of the magisterium it would be possible to make it more representative of the diversity of the church in its exercise. The collaboration between councils and university faculties of theology in the late Middle Ages and the fact that some who were not bishops participated as voting members in ecumenical councils are precedents for developing new ways to exercise the authority of the church's magisterium.

[70]See Hervé-Marie Legrand, "The Presidency of the Eucharist," p. 437.

4

Authority In The Ecumenical Dialogue

The movement to reestablish unity between the various Christian churches cannot avoid the question of authority. Some church union proposals (such as the one between Anglicans and Methodists in England) have come to grief precisely on this issue. Episcopally structured churches insist on the importance and role of the historic episcopate. Churches with a presbyteral polity resist the suggestion that they lack anything essential to the church's fundamental structure. Congregationally ordered churches distrust hierarchical authority; they stress the fundamental equality of all believers and emphasize the ultimate authority of the local congregation. If the churches are to reestablish communion, they will have to reach some agreement on the nature and place of ecclesiastical authority. Therefore authority has begun to emerge as the crucial ecumenical question.

In recent years a number of the bilateral and multilateral ecumenical consultations have addressed the question of authority. They reflect the different concerns and interests of their participating churches. Because the ecumenical consensus statements they have produced represent the closest thing to a genuinely common theology which incorporates the doctrinal positions and concerns of the different churches, these consensus statements constitute a rich resource. In what follows we will consider four of them: *The Final Report* of the Anglican-Roman Catholic International Commission (ARCIC), the Lutheran-Roman Catholic dialogue, both in the United States and on the international level, the *Baptism, Eucharist and Ministry (BEM)* text of the World Council of Churches, and the Consultation on Church Union (COCU).

Because the various statements differ in their concepts, language, and concerns, the points singled out will not always be the same. ARCIC has two statements specifically on authority; other documents approach authority more obliquely. There are common elements, but some issues must be expressed in the terms in which they are framed in the statements themselves. Of course, the question of ordained ministry is central. While authority and ordained ministry are not synonymous, it is precisely the different understandings of the nature and authority of the ordained ministry which are at issue between the churches. Consider the greater attention almost always given to ministry in any ecumenical statement. Therefore our considerations here will focus on how the ordained ministry is understood and structured.

But the broader questions relative to authority in the Christian community cannot be ignored and indeed force their way in at various points. We need to consider these too. Hopefully our review of these documents will begin to point to an emerging consensus on authority which must be incorporated into tomorrow's church.

The ARCIC Final Report

When the Bishop of Rome, Pope Paul VI, welcomed the Archbishop of Canterbury, Dr. Michael Ramsey, at St. Paul's Outside-the-Walls on March 23, 1966, their meeting marked a significant new beginning in the relationship between their two communions. In the joint statement the two church leaders issued at the conclusion of their meeting, after giving thanks to God, they declared their intentions of inaugurating "a serious dialogue founded on the Gospels and on the ancient common traditions" in the hope that this could "lead to the unity in truth for which Christ prayed."[1]

[1]Common Declaration of 24 March 1966 in *The Archbishop of Canterbury's Visit to Rome, March 1966* (Church Information Office, 1966), p. 14.

The official dialogue between the two communions resulting from this encounter proceeded in two stages. First, the Anglican-Roman Catholic Joint Preparatory Commission was set up to establish a program and priorities in the theological dialogue, and to consider matters of practical ecclesiastical cooperation. The second stage was the joint appointment in 1969 by the Pope and the Archbishop of Canterbury of the Anglican-Roman Catholic International Commission. At its first meeting at Windsor, England, in January of 1970, ARCIC agreed both on a goal of working for the "organic union" of the Roman Catholic Church and the Anglican Communion, and on a "strategy," namely that doctrinal agreement must precede practical recommendations for organic union. The agreed statements published over the following years on eucharistic doctrine (1971), ministry and ordination (1973), and authority in the church (1976, 1981) were collected and combined with a number of "elucidations" in the *Final Report*, published in 1982.[2]

The *Final Report* singles out several concepts which bring into focus the nature of authority as understood in the ARCIC consultation. They include the nature of the ordained ministry, *episcope*, conciliarity, and primacy. We will consider them in this order.

1. *The Nature of the Ordained Ministry.* The ARCIC statement *Ministry and Ordination* situates the ordained ministry within the broader context of the various ministries which are the work of the Spirit (no. 2). But it is a particular gift, bestowed upon the minister by the "sacramental act" of ordination; since God's call is irrevocable, ordination is not to be repeated (no. 15). Ordained ministers share through baptism in the common priesthood of the People of God; "Nevertheless their ministry is not an extension of the common Christian priesthood but belongs to another realm of the gifts of the Spirit" (no. 13). The statement does not intend to present an exhaustive statement on ministry; in

[2]Anglican-Roman Catholic International Commission, *The Final Report* (London: CTS/SPCK, 1982).

regard to structure, it simply notes that the threefold ministry of bishop, presbyter, and deacon emerged in its fullness after the apostolic age and then became universal in the church (no. 6).

2. *Episcope.* What is the authority of the ordained ministry? *Authority in the Church I* speaks of "the *episcope* of the ordained ministry" as a specific gift of pastoral authority which belongs primarily to the bishop (no. 5). Earlier in the dialogue the statement *Ministry and Ordination* had summarized the various New Testament images describing the ministry of leadership and unity with the concept of *episcope,* literally oversight, which it identifies as an "essential element" in the responsibility of the ordained ministry. *Episcope* is ordered toward maintaining the unity and apostolicity of the church; "This responsibility involves fidelity to the apostolic faith, its embodiment in the life of the Church today, and its transmission to the Church of tomorrow" (no. 9).

Ministry and Ordination describes *episcope* in the context of the threefold ministry: "Presbyters are joined with the bishop in his oversight of the church and in the ministry of the word and the sacraments; they are given authority to preside at the eucharist and to pronounce absolution. Deacons, though not so empowered, are associated with bishops and presbyters in the ministry of word and sacrament, and assist in oversight" (no. 9). Thus *episcope* cannot be understood as a *monarchical* function; it clearly has a *collegial* dimension.

The next three paragraphs unfold and highlight three key functions through which the oversight of the ordained ministry is exercised: in preaching the word (no. 10), in celebrating the sacraments (no. 11), and in presiding at the celebration of the Eucharist (no. 12). The statement is careful to bring out the complementarity of word and sacrament, for in "both . . . Christians meet the living God" (no. 11). At the same time there is a movement from word and sacrament to the Eucharist, the church's "central act of worship" (no. 12), so fundamental to the church's life "that the essential nature of the Christian ministry, however this may be expressed, is most clearly seen in its celebration" (no. 13). In paragraphs 12 and 13 the sacramental nature of *episcope* emerges. As Herbert Ryan has emphasized, it cannot be reduced to a merely sociological function: "Oversight . . . in the Christian community is as sacramental as the community itself is.[3]

3. *Conciliarity. Authority in the Church I* treats both conciliarity and primacy as complementary elements of *episcope* which need to be kept in a proper balance (no. 22). It traces the conciliar principle back as far as the "Council" of Jerusalem (Acts 15), the earliest example of different churches coming together to resolve matters of mutual concern. Councils can be regional or worldwide, and they can be composed of bishops alone or of bishops, clergy, and laity. Decisions arrived at by "ecumenical" councils are binding on the whole church (no. 9).

The document seems to speak of conciliarity in either an historical or an ideal sense; it describes how authority is exercised and judgments are made in "times of crisis" (no. 19). The church's bishops are "collectively responsible for defending the apostolic faith" (no. 20) and "share in a special gift of Christ" in carrying out their conciliar responsibilities (no. 19). A footnote to paragraph 19 points out that the Roman Catholic Church has continued to hold general councils of its bishops while the Anglican Communion has developed other forms of conciliarity.[4] Perhaps in response to the charge that the Commission had neglected the role of the laity (*Elucidation* no. 14), *Authority in the Church II* suggests that conciliarity should involve lay participation. It affirms that the church needs "a multiple dispersed authority, with which all God's people are actively involved" as well as a universal primate (no. 33).

---

[3]Herbert J. Ryan, "The Canterbury Statement on Ministry and Ordination," *Worship* 48 (1974) 19.

[4]An interesting article by Gavin White suggests that neither collegiality nor conciliarity properly describe Anglican governing structures such as the Primates' Meeting, the Lambeth Conference, and the Anglican Consultative Council since they lack juridical authority. See his "Collegiality and Conciliarity in the Anglican Communion," in *Authority in the Anglican Communion*, ed. Stephen W. Sykes (Toronto: Anglican Book Centre, 1987), pp. 202-220.

4. *Primacy*. Another form of *episcope* is represented by primacy. According to *Authority in the Church I* the concept has its origins in the early church practice of assigning to the bishop of a prominent see the responsibility of watching over the other bishops in his region (no. 10). Primacy is exercised on different levels. The *Elucidation* (no. 7) mentions the roles of metropolitans and patriarchs, as well as new forms such as elected presidents of episcopal conferences in the Roman Catholic Church and certain elected primates in the Anglican Communion.

The primacy of the bishop of Rome also developed historically; over the centuries it has received different theological interpretations and its image has sometimes been overloaded or obscured. The document emphasizes this universal primacy as a ministry of unity: "Yet the primacy, rightly understood, implies that the bishop of Rome exercises his oversight in order to guard and promote the faithfulness of all the churches to Christ and one another. Communion with him is intended as a safeguard of the catholicity of each local church, and as a sign of the communion of all the churches" (no. 14).

Recognizing the see of Rome as the only see which makes a claim to a universal primacy and continues to exercise this kind of *episcope*, *Authority in the Church I* states: "It seems appropriate that in any future union a universal primacy such as has been described should be held by that see" (no. 23). Its argument for a universal primacy in the church tomorrow is not simply historical; the *Elucidation* no. 8 notes the conviction that God wills a visible unity for the church and that maintaining such unity at the universal level "includes the *episcope* of a universal primate." For the Commission this is a doctrinal statement. *Authority in the Church II* repeated this; it stressed that a Christian community could be recognized as church without being in communion with the see of Rome (no. 12). But by stating its belief that "the primacy of the bishop of Rome can be affirmed as part of God's design for the universal *koinonia*" (no. 15) the Commission also recognized the claim of Vatican I that the Roman primacy exists by divine right (*jure divino*).

The primacy affirmed by *Authority in the Church II* is a carefully qualified one. The universal primate should exercise his authority collegially with his brother bishops; he is not the source of their authority (no. 19); there are moral limits to the exercise of his authority (no. 20); Anglicans are entitled to an assurance that acknowledging the universal primacy of the bishop of Rome would not be at the cost of their own theological, liturgical, and other particular traditions (no. 22).[5] While the document recognizes that the church exercises teaching authority through universal councils and that in a future united church the universal primate must be able to speak with authority (no. 25), ARCIC prefers to speak of its "belief in the preservation of the Church from error" rather than to use the term infallibility (no. 32).

The *Final Report* concludes by expressing the hope that "significant initiatives" will be taken to bring both churches along the way toward their ultimate goal of full communion.

The Lutheran-Roman Catholic Dialogue

The Lutheran-Roman Catholic dialogue has taken place on two levels, one international, the other in the United States. The origins of the dialogue in the United States can be traced back to an informal meeting in 1963 between then Bishop John J. Wright of Pittsburgh and Dr. Paul C. Empie, the executive director of the National Lutheran Council. Two years later the idea of a dialogue between the two confessions was formally approved by the National Lutheran Council, acting in its capacity as the U.S.A. National Committee of the Lutheran World Federation.[6] The LWF gave its concurrence. On the Roman Catholic side, approval came from the Bishops' Committee for Ecumenical and Interre-

---

[5] J. Robert Wright points out the need for some limiting definitions of papal jurisdiction in "Papal Authority in the Light of Recent Developments," in Sykes, *Authority in the Anglican Communion*, pp. 236-263.

[6] At this time the Lutheran World Federation included the American Lutheran Church and the Lutheran Church in America. The Lutheran Church-Missouri Synod, while not a member of the LWF, was invited to send two representatives to the dialogue.

ligious Affairs (BCEIA), a committee of the National Conference of Catholic Bishops. Representatives of the two
groups met in Baltimore, March 1965, to do the preparatory
work for the dialogue.

The group which resulted represents the two committees
which appointed it. Its official status carries neither the
weight nor the dignity of the Anglican-Roman Catholic
International Commission, appointed jointly by Pope Paul
VI and the Archbishop of Canterbury, Dr. Michael Ramsey.
And unlike ARCIC, whose stated goal is the "organic union"
of the two communions, the U.S. Lutheran-Roman Catholic
Dialogue is more an exploratory encounter, seeking to dis-
cover areas of agreement through doctrinal discussion. Since
1965, seven major agreed statements have been published:
The Status of the Nicene Creed as Dogma of the Church
(1965), *One Baptism for the Remission of Sins* (1966), *The
Eucharist as Sacrifice* (1967), *Eucharist and Ministry* (1970),
Papal Primacy and the Universal Church (1974), *Teaching
Authority and Infallibility in the Church* (1978), and *Justif-
ication by Faith* (1985).[7]

On the international level, what became known as the
international Roman Catholic-Lutheran Joint Commission
developed out of some meetings during the Second Vatican
Council between council fathers and theologians and ob-
servers from the Lutheran World Federation.[8] As a result of
these contacts, some further conversations between the
Vatican Secretariat for Promoting Christian Unity and the
LWF led to the formation of Roman Catholic-Lutheran
Working Group which met twice between August 1965 and
April 1966. In 1967 a joint study commission on "The Gospel
and the Church" was formed; with the publication of its

---

[7]These have been published in a series under the general title *Lutherans and
Catholics in Dialogue*; volumes I-IV were published jointly by the United States
Catholic Conference and the United States National Committee of the Lutheran
World Federation; volumes V-VII were published by Augsburg Publishing House,
Minneapolis.

[8]See Harding Meyer, "Roman Catholic/Lutheran Dialogue," *One in Christ* 22
(1986) 146-168.

report in 1972 (the Malta Report) the first phase in the dialogue came to a conclusion.[9]

In 1973 the Working Group was reconstituted as the Roman Catholic-Lutheran Joint Commission. Beyond the charting of doctrinal consensus between the two churches, the Joint Commisssion set itself the task of attempting to find ways to translate agreement into practical steps towards reconciliation. Over the years the following documents were produced: "The Eucharist" (1978), "All under one Christ" (1980), "Ways to Community" (1980), "The Ministry in the Church" (1981),[10] "Reciprocal Admission to the Eucharist" (completed in 1982 but not yet published because it lacks unanimous endorsement by the Catholic participants), "Martin Luther-Witness to Jesus Christ" (1983), and "Facing Unity" (1985).[11]

These different Lutheran-Roman Catholic dialogues have proceeded with different agendas and have not always covered the sames issues; for example, the international dialogue has yet to address specifically the question of the papacy. It cannot automatically be assumed that a position taken by one will also represent the position of the other. Nevertheless it is possible to select from these dialogues certain themes touching on our general subject of authority. Several have emerged which we will consider in roughly the order that they appear in the dialogues; the nature of the ordained ministry, papal primacy, teaching authority, and the historic episcopate.

1. *The Nature of the Ordained Ministry.* In 1970 the Lutheran-Catholic Dialogue in the United States published *Lutherans and Catholics in Dialogue IV: Eucharist and Ministry.*[12] The statement begins by distinguishing between

[9]The Malta Report was published in *Growth in Agreement: Reports and Agreed Statements of Ecumenical Conversations on a World Level*, ed. Harding Meyer and Lukas Vischer (New York: Paulist Press, 1984), pp. 168-189.

[10]These documents can be found in *Growth in Agreement*, pp. 190-275.

[11]Both published in *Facing Unity: Models, Forms and Phases of Catholic-Lutheran Church Fellowship* (Geneva: Lutheran World Federation, 1985).

[12]*Lutherans and Catholics in Dialogue IV: Eucharist and Ministry*, ed. Paul C. Empie and T. Austin Murphy (Washington: USCC, 1970).

"ministry" as the "task or service of the whole church" and "the (or a) Ministry [upper case], a particular form of service—a specific order, function or gift (charism) within and for the sake of Christ's church in its mission to the world" (no. 9). The ambiguities and tortured syntax of this sentence reflect the underlying differences in approach of the two traditions. This special ministry has the task of "proclaiming God's Word, administering the sacraments, exhorting and reproving" (no. 13). After pointing out that Catholics understand ordination as a sacramental act and Lutheran practice "shows a conviction concerning the sacramental reality of ordination" (no. 16), the statement affirms that "entry into this apostolic and God-given Ministry is by ordination ... [which] is for a lifetime of service and is not to be repeated (no. 18).

In regard to the structure of the ordained ministry, the statement points out that the Lutheran tradition "has one order of ordained Ministers, usually called pastors, which combines features of the episcopate and the presbyterate"; the pastor "corresponds in his functions with the bishop in the Catholic tradition" (no. 21). In their reflections the Lutheran participants point out that the Lutheran reformers wanted to preserve episcopal polity, but that "As long as the ordained Ministry is retained, any form of polity which serves the proclamation of the gospel is acceptable" (no. 28). We will turn to the question of the historic episcopate below.

2. *Papal Primacy.* The U.S. dialogue next turned to the question of papal primacy.[13] Despite some initial misgivings about tackling such a thorny and emotionally loaded issue, the introduction to the statement notes that the participants once again found common ground: "There is a growing awareness among Lutherans of the necessity of a specific Ministry to serve the church's unity and universal mission, while Catholics increasingly see the need for a more nuanced understanding of the role of the papacy within the universal

---

[13] *Lutherans and Catholics in Dialogue V: Papal Primacy and the Universal Church,* ed. Paul C. Empie and T. Austin Murphy (Minneapolis: Augsburg Publishing House, 1974).

church." Both of these points were developed in their statement.

A focus on various means of unifying the universal church historically and in particular a consideration of the image of Peter in the New Testament led to the use of the term "Petrine function . . . *a particular form of Ministry exercised by a person, officeholder, or local church with reference to the church as a whole.* This Petrine function of the Ministry serves to promote or preserve the oneness of the church by symbolizing unity, and by facilitating communications, mutual assistance or correction, and collaboration in the church's mission" (no. 4). Though not the only example of this function, the statement points out that the "single most notable representative of the Ministry toward the church universal, both in duration and geographical scope, has been the bishop of Rome" (no. 5).

The approach to this ministry of the bishop of Rome is quite nuanced. The statement points out how the understanding of the historical issues has changed: "The question whether Jesus appointed Peter the first pope has shifted in modern scholarship to the question of the extent to which the subsequent use of the images of Peter in reference to the papacy is consistent with the thrust of the New Testament" (no. 13). Historical studies illustrate how the forms of the papacy have been adapted to different historical periods (no. 21). A renewal of papal structure for the future would have to respect three principles: the legitimate diversity of the churches in piety, liturgy, theology, custom and law; collegiality in the area of government so that all levels of the church can share in the responsibility of leadership; and subsidiarity, which by insisting that decisions which can be made on lower levels not be made by higher authorities safeguards legitimate freedom, full participation, and the rights of minorities (nos. 22-25).

The statement suggest that in the future "the pope's service to unity in relation to the Lutheran churches would be more pastoral than juridical" (no. 28). Though they acknowledge that there are remaining disagreements, at the end of the statement the participants ask the Lutheran churches "if they are able to acknowledge not only the legitimacy of the papal

Ministry in the service of the Roman Catholic communion but even the possibility and the desirability of the papal Ministry, renewed under the gospel and committed to Christian freedom, in a larger communion which would include the Lutheran churches" (no. 32).

The 1981 International RC/L Joint Commission statement, "The Ministry in the Church," did not deal with the question of the papacy directly, but it noted that the question of a ministry to the unity of the church does arise along with reflections on the episcopacy (no. 67) and that in the dialogues the possibility of a Petrine office of the bishop of Rome, subordinated to the gospel, reinterpreted, and restructured need not be excluded by Lutherans (no. 73).

3. *Teaching Authority.* When the dialogue turned to the question of teaching authority and infallibility,[14] the Lutheran participants acknowledged that they "were prepared for disappointments"; however what they discovered was that infallibility was not "a solely Roman Catholic problem" (LR 2). The Common Statement reexamines the question of infallibility in the broader context of the whole question of doctrinal authority. With the aid of modern historical studies in Scripture and the church fathers, the dialogue participants discovered that they were "able to think in ways which are different from earlier discussions" (CS 4). They acknowledge that Lutherans and Catholics "now speak in increasingly similar ways about the gospel and its communication, about the authority of Christian truth, and about how to settle disputes concerning the understanding of the Christian message" (CS 41).

Lutherans and Catholics are agreed that Jesus Christ is the Lord of the church who discloses his sovereignty through the proclamation of the Gospel and the administration of the sacraments; that the Word of God in Scripture is nor-

---

[14] *Lutherans and Catholics in Dialogue VI: Teaching Authority and Infallibility in the Church*, ed. Paul C. Empie, T. Austin Murphy, and Joseph A. Burgess (Minneapolis: Augsburg Publishing House, 1978); the statement is comprised of three parts, each with separately number paragraphs: I. Common Statement; II. Roman Catholic Reflections; III. Lutheran Reflections. In citing the parts of the document I will refer to them by the initials CS, RCR, and LR respectively.

mative for all proclamation and teaching; that the Word of God is transmitted in the apostolic tradition, which itself is interpreted "with the assistance of tradition in the form of creeds, liturgies, dogma, confessions, doctrines, forms of church government and discipline, and patterns of devotion and service." They are agreed that there are ministries and structures charged with teaching, supervision, and coordination with the responsibility "to judge doctrine and condemn doctrine that is contrary to the Gospel"; that "there may appropriately be a Ministry in the universal Church charged with primary responsibility for the unity of the people of God in their mission to the world"; that this ministry "includes a responsibility for overseeing both the church's proclamation and, where necessary, the reformulation of doctrine in fidelity to the Scriptures" (CS 41).

The foregoing convergences do not yet indicate full agreement on the question of teaching authority. The statement points out that the Lutheran churches are deficient in not having the structures to exercise a universal magisterium: "Lutherans, like other Christians in our present divided state, lack the institutional means to participate with other Christian traditions in doctrinal decision-making. Thus they are confronted with the increasingly urgent need to develop new structures or adapt old ones in a way that will do justice to this universal aspect of their responsibility to the gospel" (CS 46). The international RC/L Joint Commission also speaks of the Lutheran churches as being "confronted with the need to rethink the problem of the teaching office and the teaching authority," especially in connection with the episcopal ministry ("The Ministry in the Church" no. 56).

On the other hand, Lutherans still regard Catholics as overconfidently identifying the presence of the Holy Spirit in the church with one particular person or office, and together with many Catholics "believe that the doctrine and practice of papal teaching authority are not yet sufficiently protected against abuses." (CS 42).

Most important is the growing agreement on the practice of teaching authority. Both affirm the supreme authority of the Gospel, and neither can continue to insist onesidedly on church structures, tradition, or "Scripture alone" as the

uniquely sufficient source for the transmission and interpretation of the Gospel. A growing recognition of the need
to restructure teaching authority in both traditions emerges.
Lutherans need to develop the structures to participate in a
universal magisterium. Catholics need to acknowledge more
adequately the ways in which the whole church—laity, theologians and bishops—participate in the definition of doctrine.
The statement does not arrive at more than partial agreement
(CS 58). Yet in relocating infallibility within the broader
context of teaching authority in general, the statement has
clarified the issues involved for both traditions and led to a
surprising consensus on the place and nature of magisterial
authority in the church.

4. *The Historic Episcopate.* The question of the episcopal
office as a specific issue has always been present in the
Lutheran-Catholic dialogues, but it has begun to surface
with increasing urgency. The 1980 document of the international RC/L Joint Commission, "Ways to Community,"
broaches the question of the historical episcopacy in the
context of its responsibility for church unity. It speaks of the
need for a ministry beyond that of the local congregation
with pastoral responsibility for church unity:

> Although Lutherans do not regard the historic episcopacy
> as based on an explicit irrevocable command from the
> Lord valid for all times and situations, yet this polity
> arose through the work of the Holy Spirit, and there are
> historical and ecumenical reasons for seriously considering
> its restoration in Lutheran churches (no. 23).

A ministry serving the unity of the church as a whole is in
accord with the Lord's will, even if its concrete form has not
been fixed once for all (no. 23). Towards the end of the
document the question is raised of a "possible mutual readiness to enter the fellowship of the historic episcopacy or of
the Petrine office" (no. 88) as well as a call for "institutionalized cooperation between the leaders of both churches" as
a step towards a common episcopacy (no. 89).

The 1981 document "The Ministry in the Church" was

developed with special reference to the episcopacy, seeing lack of agreement here as an obstacle to Lutheran Catholic communion (no. 2). Though the starting point for considering all ministry in the church is the common priesthood of all the baptized (no. 15), the authority of the ordained ministry is christologically based (no. 22) and cannot be understood as delegated by the community (no. 23). This statement also mentions the desire of the Lutheran reformers to retain the episcopal polity of the church and speaks of the installation of ministers by non-episcopal ministers in the 16th century as an "emergency situation" (no. 42).

Several points in regard to the mutual recognition of ministries seem especially significant in this document. The first is the Catholic emphasis that apostolic succession in the episcopal office serves to maintain the communion of the catholic and apostolic church rather than being understood primarily as an unbroken chain of ordinations (no. 62), behind which lies the old transmission of power argument. Secondly, in interpreting the Second Vatican Council on ministry in the Reformation churches, the document argues that the *defectus* in the sacrament of orders in the Reformation churches referred to by the *Decree on Ecumenism* no. 22, could be understood as meaning "a lack of the fullness of the church's ministry" rather than as a complete absence of it (no. 77).

Finally, Lutheranism approaches the question of the mutual recognition of ministries differently. According to the Augsburg Confession VII it is sufficient [*satis est*] for the unity of the church that the gospel be preached in its purity and the sacraments be rightly administered (nos. 79-80). This is interpreted not as a final statement, but as a basic one which, when so understood, can free Lutherans to ask what form of church structure could most effectively support the life and mission of the church and also "to face up to the call for communion with the historic episcopal office" (No. 80).

If communion with the historical episcopacy is seen as a possibility in the 1981 document on ministry, the 1985 document *Facing Unity* acknowledges it as a need, but only as part of the process of the mutual recognition of ministry. The document stresses that the lack of the sacrament of orders claimed by the Catholic side cannot be overcome by theological agreements or ecclesiastical decisions; "What is needed, rather, is acceptance of the fellowship in ecclesial ministry, and this, ultimately, means acceptance of the fellowship in episcopal ministry which stands in apostolic succession" (no. 98).

The document presents a phased process which could lead to a common ordained ministry and to fellowship in the episcopal office. First, there should be some preliminary forms of the joint exercise of *episcope*, realized through joint working groups, mutual participation in church synods, working relationships between church leaders, and common consultations and decisions (nos. 120-122).

Second, with a fundamental consensus on faith and sacraments, there should be a mutual act of recognition of ministry. The Catholic side would affirm the presence of the ministry instituted by Christ in the Lutheran churches "while at the same time pointing to a lack of fullness of the ordained ministry as a *defectus* which, for the sake of church fellowship, has jointly to be overcome" (no. 124).

Third, the two traditions will begin to exercise a single *episcope* in collegial form; this will include joint ordinations (no. 127).

Finally, the joint exercise of episcopal authority particularly in ordaining would lead over time to the development of a common ordained ministry (no. 132) with an episcopal authority which could be expressed in several different forms: a single *episcope* in collegial form, a single bishop for both communities, or the merger of communities into a single church under a single bishop (nos. 142-145). This last case might be appropriate in a non-Christian environment where both churches find themselves in a minority status.

The document implies several times that the episcopal office must be reformed. The exercise of authority by church leaders does not exclude the responsibility of the laity or the principle of synodal or conciliar government (no. 112). Furthermore, the doctrinal decisions of church authorities need to be received by local churches, congregations, and believers (no. 60). The need to reform the way authority is exercised needs to be emphasized and will take time. But in presenting a proposal for a reconciliation between the Roman Catholic and Lutheran churches which would include fellowship in the historic episcopal office and eventually a common ministry, the international Roman Catholic-Lutheran Joint Commission has broken new ground.

The WCC Baptism, Eucharist and Ministry Text

The modern ecumenical movement was born, not at the Second Vatican Council at Rome in 1962 but at the World Missionary Conference which met at Edinburgh, Scotland, in 1910. And it arose as an impulse within that part of the church which organizationally has been the most divided, Protestantism.[15] The Conference at Edinburgh was an outgrowth of the Nineteenth Century missionary movement which in the spirit of the Gospel sought to make all nations disciples of Christ. Its focus was unity, not yet as an end in itself, but as a means to evangelism. It sought unity for the advancement of the mission of the church through cooperation between the churches in the distribution of the Bible, in education, in the production and circulation of Christian literature, and in confronting the common problems of evangelism.

Edinburgh was a Protestant conference. Representatives of the Roman Catholic Church and the Orthodox churches had not been invited and probably would not have come if they had been. Yet the conference was a training ground for those who would be leaders in the ecumenical movement, among them John R. Mott, Joseph H. Oldham, and William Temple. And from the new sense of fellowship experienced here among Christians was to issue the World Conference on Faith and Order, with its first meeting at Lausanne in 1927, and ultimately, the first assembly of the World Council of Churches at Amsterdam in 1948.

The unanimous acceptance of the text *Baptism, Eucharist*

---

[15]See Kenneth Scott Latourette, "Ecumenical Bearings of the Missionary Movement and the International Missionary Council," in *A History of the Ecumenical Movement, 1517-1948*, ed. Ruth Rouse and Stephen Charles Neill (Philadelphia: Westminster Press, 1968), pp. 351-402.

and Ministry at the meeting of the Faith and Order Commission in Lima, Peru, in January 1982 marks the culmination of fifty years of reflection on these themes by the Commission.[16] The text represents a "convergence" of thinking on the part of the members of the Commission, which now includes Orthodox theologians and some Roman Catholics, even though the Roman Catholic Church is not yet a member of the WCC. It must still be received by the member churches to stand as a genuine consensus. But as the Preface notes, "That theologians of such widely different traditions should be able to speak so harmoniously about baptism, eucharist and ministry is unprecedented in the modern ecumenical movement."[17] In BEM the issue of authority emerges in the statement on ministry. We will consider authority in the context of ministry, *episkope*, the structure of the ordained ministry, the historic episcopate, and the reform of structures.

1. *Authority and Ordained Ministry.* BEM understands the ordained ministry as one among the many charisms entrusted to the church. The authority of this ministry is christologically/pneumatically grounded; it is from Christ but mediated through the Holy Spirit present in the community. Thus ordained ministry cannot be understood apart from the calling of the whole People of God (M no. 15).

The BEM text seeks to balance the authority it recognizes in the ordained ministry by emphasizing the need for the ordained minister to exercise authority in a responsive and collaborative way: "Only when they seek the response and acknowledgment of the community can their authority be protected from the distortions of isolation and domination" (M no. 16). At this point the Commentary points out the dangers of exercising authority without regard for the community, or conversely, of so reducing authority that ordained ministers become dependent on the common opinion of the community (Commentary no. 16).

The tradition of ordaining in the context of the Eucharist brings out that ordination is an act of the whole community;

---

[16]WCC, *Baptism, Eucharist and Ministry* (Geneva: WCC, 1982).
[17]Ibid., Preface, p. ix.

performed by the laying on of hands by those appointed, ordination is a "sacramental sign" as well as an acknowledgment of gifts and commitment (no.41). It is not repeated (no. 48).

2. *Episkope.* BEM introduces *episkope* in the context of the Eucharist; the Commentary to paragraph no. 14 notes that presiding over the Eucharist is *"intimately related to the task of guiding the community, i.e. supervising its life (episkope) and strengthening its vigilance in relation to the truth of the apostolic message"*; thus it is appropriate that the ordained minister should have the task of eucharistic presidency (M Com. no. 14).

Episkope or supervision is rooted in the New Testament; the apostles exercised it over the whole church; later Timothy and Titus exercised it over a given area, and still later bishops began to exercise *episkope* over several local communities (M no. 21). Among the other gifts and ministries, "a ministry of *episkope* is necessary to express and safeguard the unity of the body" and every church needs it in some form (M no. 23).

3. *The Structure of the Ordained Ministry.* Although the New Testament does not prescribe a single pattern of ministry BEM notes that the threefold pattern of bishop, presbyter, and deacon emerged in the context of the local eucharistic community and became established throughout the church in the second and third centuries (M nos. 19-20). And it suggests that it may serve as a means towards and expression of unity today (M. nos. 22, 25).

The function of bishops is to "preach the Word, preside at the sacraments, and administer discipline in such a way as to be representative pastoral ministers of oversight, continuity and unity in the Church" (M no. 29). Presbyters "serve as pastoral ministers of Word and sacraments in a local eucharistic community" (M no. 30). Deacons represent the church's role as servant in the world; their liturgical responsibilities show the interdependence of worship and service. They may be elected to responsibilities for governance (M no. 31).

4. *The Historic Episcopate.* BEM argues that the succession of bishops became one of the ways in which the apostolic tradition of the church was expressed, and that it was understood as "serving, symbolizing and guarding the continuity of the apostolic faith and communion" (M no. 36). Thus it sees the episcopal succession "as a sign, though not a guarantee, of the continuity and unity of the Church" (M no. 38), and it suggests that those churches which lack it may need "to recover the sign of the episcopal succession" (M no. 53b). What it cannot accept is the idea that a ministry should be invalid until it enters the line of the episcopal succession (no. 38). Thus BEM offers a nuanced argument for the recovery of the historic episcopate.

5. *The Reform of Structures.* The text calls attention to the need to exercise the ordained ministry in a *personal, collegial,* and *communal* way. It should be personal, to effectively point to the presence of Christ among his people. The term collegial emphasizes that ordained ministers belong to a college sharing a common task; they must work together. To speak of a communal dimension to the exercise of ordained ministry is to underline the need for the "community's effective participation in the discovery of God's will and the guidance of the Spirit" (M no. 26). If there is a need for a ministry of unity at both local and regional levels, the text also stresses that all members should be able to participate in the life and decision-making of the community either actively or through "representative synodal gatherings" (M no. 27). Geoffrey Wainwright says that this synodal experience may be one of the main contributions of the more "protestant" churches.[18]

BEM challenges the ways in which authority is exercised in both Catholic and Protestant churches. Protestant churches will have to consider its argument for the recovery of episcopal succession. The Roman Catholic Church and the Orthodox churches will have to consider carefully the

---

[18]Geoffrey Wainwright, "Reconciliation in Ministry," in *Ecumenical Perspectives on Baptism, Eucharist and Ministry,* ed. Max Thurian (Geneva: WCC, 1983), p. 132.

case it makes for recognizing non-episcopally ordained ministries as real ministries of word and sacrament with "apostolic content" (M no. 53a), its call for a reform of the traditional threefold ministry to make it more personal, collegial, and communal (M nos. 24-27), and its openness to the ordination of women (M no. 54).

There are some areas in which the document will have to be improved. Some Roman Catholic commentators have criticized it for failing to develop more adequately the collegial responsibility of the episcopal office for maintaining the communion of the universal church[19] and for its virtual silence on the teaching authority of bishops.[20] On the other hand it has been objected that BEM is "too Catholic" in its approach to ministry, though as Joseph Eagan has observed, BEM's intention in the statement on ministry "is not to canonize Orthodox or Catholic or Anglican theology and practice today but rather to recover the convictions and life of the sub-apostolic church and the church of the great ecumenical councils and of the fathers as these developed from the church of the New Testament."[21] It is true that the BEM text on ministry represents only the ecumenical convergences formulated by the Faith and Order Commission. But if the various churches to which it has been submitted are able to recognize in it their own faith it can become the basis for a substantial agreement on those issues of ministry and authority which have traditionally divided the churches.

The COCU Consensus

In December of 1960 Eugene Carson Blake, a Presbyterian, preached a sermon in San Francisco's Grace Cathedral

[19]See the remarks of the Research Team appointed by the Catholic Theological Society of America in "A Global Evaluation of *Baptism, Eucharist and Ministry*" in *Catholic Perspectives on Baptism, Eucharist and Ministry*, ed. Michael A. Fahey (Lanham, MD: University Press of America, 1986), p. 24.

[20]William Marrevee, "Lima Document on Ordained Ministry," in *Catholic Perspectives on BEM*, p. 175.

[21]Joseph F. Eagan, "Ordained Ministry in BEM: A Theological Critique," *The Ecumenical Review* 36 (1984) 273-274.

(Episcopal Church) which was to have profound ecumenical consequences.[22] Blake suggested that the Episcopal Church and the United Presbyterians join with the Methodist Church and the United Church of Christ in discussions aimed at the formation of a united church "both catholic and reformed." An initial meeting in 1962 resulted in the establishment of what was called the "Consultation on Church Union." COCU, as it came to be known, grew rapidly to include nine churches; the African Methodist Episcopal Church, the African Methodist Episcopal Zion Church, the Christian Church (Disciples of Christ), the Christian Methodist Episcopal Church, the Episcopal Church, the International Council of Community Churches, the Presbyterian Church (U.S.A.), the United Church of Christ, and the United Methodist Church."

Of the thirty or so church union efforts throughout the world COCU is one of the most important. In terms of the memberships and polities represented, it is one of the most diverse. The participation from the beginning of three predominantly black churches has given COCU a sensitivity for inclusiveness which has broadened beyond race issues to include a concern for women and the handicapped, and ultimately, to the recognition that whatever divides and separates the human community is an ecumenical problem with theological implications. Finally COCU has emphasized the experience of growing into Christian unity on the local level through racially and confessionally inclusive experiments in Christian life, mission, and worship. Open to the responses of its participating churches, COCU has gone through several phases or stages in its pursuit of its goal, a Church of Christ Uniting.

The first phase in COCU's history covers the decade from 1962 to 1972. This beginning phase included the organization of the Consultation and its initial efforts to develop a theological basis for union, a growing awareness of racism as a church-dividing issue, the publication of *A Plan of Union*

[22]For a historical overview of COCU and basic bibliography see John A. Rodano, "Consultation on Church Union: Recent Developments, New Directions," in *Religious Studies Review* 11 (1985) 151-159.

for the Church of Christ Uniting in 1970,[23] and subsequent evaluation of the responses to this document.

The *Plan of Union*, really a draft, was an ambitious document which suggested the formation of a single united church with a single system of government and a unified episcopal office. Thus it followed the model of full organic unity.[24] Though the churches did not formally vote on the plan, their responses indicated a clear rejection. The United Presbyterians actually withdrew from COCU for a year. The churches clearly were not yet ready to enter into organic union. Yet the considerable agreement reached on issues of faith, worship, and the basic nature of the ministry was an encouraging sign.

The second phase, beginning in 1973, shifted the approach somewhat. While the work of refining the theological consensus continued, the Consultation began to work towards creating a greater experience of unity from below. The churches were encouraged to develop ways of sharing life and worship through inclusive groups known as "Generating Communities" and "Interim Eucharistic Fellowships." The emphasis was on "living our way towards unity." At the same time more attention was given to the concerns of middle level church judicatories or administrators whose interest or indifference would be crucial.

During this period also COCU developed its characteristic inclusive and socially engaged orientation. A number of "alerts" on church-dividing issues such as racism, sexism, and handicapism led to further study and the incorporation of these concerns into the document that ultimately emerged. Gerald F. Moede, General Secretary of COCU, has suggested that "one of COCU's enduring contributions to the church union movement is its identification of such issues as theological, and its attempts to begin to rectify them through

---

[23]*A Plan of Union for the Church of Christ Uniting* (Princeton, New Jersey: COCU, 1970).

[24]See Stuart G. Leyden, "An Appeal for Federal Union: An American Model of Church Union With Ecumenical Horizons," *Journal of Ecumenical Studies* 20 (1983) 276.

intentional compensatory policies before union."[25]

The third phase in COCU's existence can be dated from 1982 when COCU's Louisville Plenary affirmed as a "next step" towards unity the covenantal principle which Moede had suggested two years earlier. Rather than focus on a single church, Moede proposed that churches could enter into mutually agreed upon covenants as an interim step for joining in life and mission while they sought to learn from experience what the ultimate form of visible unity might look like.[26]

The theological consensus revised from *A Plan Of Union* was expressed in a document entitled *The COCU Consensus: In Quest of a Church of Christ Uniting*, first published in 1976, revised between 1980 and 1984 on the basis of suggestions made by the churches, and finally approved and commended to the churches by a Plenary session at Baltimore in 1984.[27] *The COCU Consensus* document benefits from its appearing after the WCC *Baptism, Eucharist and Ministry* text; it acknowledges its debt to BEM at certain points in its section on ministry. The document consists of seven chapters which address, 1. the problem of division and goal of unity; 2. the kind of unity sought; 3. moving towards a church catholic, evangelical, and reformed; 4. membership; 5. expressions of the church's confession of faith: 6. worship; and 7. ministry. It claims to be a consensus statement, if somewhat "proleptically," trusting that it will eventually become so (Preface).

Chapter VII on Ministry is the longest in *The COCU Consensus* document. It begins with a note that indicates that though its treatment of ministry may be different from what is presently found in the participating churches, the statement is not presenting a constitution; it is offering a sketch which will have to be later filled out in the Councils of

---

[25]Cited by Rodano, "Consultation on Church Union: Recent Developments," p. 155.

[26]See *Convenanting Toward Unity: From Consensus to Communion* (Princeton, New Jersey: COCU, 1985).

[27]*The COCU Consensus: In Quest of a Church of Christ Uniting,* ed. Gerald F. Moede (Princeton, New Jersey: COCU, 1985).

Oversight, the "initial bridges" which will be thrown across the chasms presently separating the churches from each other. We will consider authority and the ordained ministry, the structure of the ministry, *episcope*, the historic episcopate, and a new term, governance.

1. *Authority and Ordained Ministry. The COCU Consensus* treats both ordained and lay ministries as differing and complementary forms of the one ministry of Christ (no. 21). The document adopts the language of BEM to argue that all ministries, lay and ordained, are to be understood as personal, collegial, and communal (no, 22). All are called to ministry through their baptism (no. 24); therefore baptism is understood as the basic sacrament of ministry.

The various ministries of the ordained are set within the one ministry of the whole People; "God calls forth in the Church particular ministries of persons to serve the People through proclamation of the Word and administration of the sacraments" (no. 30). Since ordained men and women share in the one ministry of the whole People, the specific character of ordained ministry is described as representative; they "symbolize and focus the ministry of Christ and the apostles as well as the ministry of the whole Church" (no. 30). "Their ordination marks them as persons who represent to the Church its own identity and mission in Jesus Christ" (no. 31). Like baptism, ordination is not repeated (no. 37).

2. *The Structure of the Ministry.* While the document acknowledges that the New Testament cannot offer an exclusive warrant for any particular ordering of ordained ministry and is sensitive to different historical developments, it sees the threefold ministry of bishop, presbyter, and deacon as predominant (no. 39). Like BEM it argues that this ministry "may nevertheless serve today as an expression of the unity we seek and as a means for achieving it" (no. 42). Also like BEM, it argues the need to reform the threefold ministry, to make leadership more collegial and to better express the service role of deacons which has too often been reduced to their liturgical functions (no. 43).

3. *Episcope. The COCU Consensus* brings out clearly the role of bishops as overseers of the church's life and symbols of its unity; it defines them as "representative pastoral ministers of oversight, unity, and continuity in the Church" through their preaching, presiding, and administering of discipline (no. 45). They are "a sign of, and are particularly responsible for, the continuity of the whole Church's Tradition ... as well as of its pastoral oversight ... as they teach the apostolic faith" (no. 46). Their responsibility as teachers of the faith is exercised "corporately and individually" (no. 51b). They have "general pastoral oversight" for all in their dioceses or jurisdictions (no. 51c). And as servants of unity they have an obligation "to call the churches to the goal of visible unity in one faith and one eucharistic fellowship" (no. 51g--quoting the Constitution of the WCC, III). Presbyters are described as pastoral overseers (no. 58d) and deacons as partners in congregational oversight (no. 63b).

4. *The Historic Episcopate.* While noting that some churches have a succession of ministers who combine the functions of both bishop and presbyter, *The COCU Consensus* commits itself to a recovery of the historic episcopate: "The participating churches intend that in the Church Uniting bishops shall stand in continuity with the historic ministry of bishops as that ministry has been maintained through the ages, and will ordain its bishops in such a way that recognition of this ministry is invited from all parts of the universal Church" (no. 48).

5. *Governance. The COCU Consensus* acknowledges that it seeks to incorporate "catholic" and "protestant" concerns as well as the experience of its different polities in its approach to ministry (no. 22). This is perhaps most evident in its emphasis on shared government: "Lay persons, bishops, presbyters, and deacons share in the governance of the Church locally, regionally, and nationally" (No. 26f). In reviewing BEM's description of ministry—here in the context of all ministries—as personal, collegial, and communal, the document expands the principle of collegiality beyond its traditional meaning; for COCU collegiality refers to the relationships between those in different ministries as well as

between those in the same ministry. Collegiality means "shared responsibility" and a "partnership in governance" which involves clergy and laity together (no. 22b).

There is a strong congregationalist element in the COCU statement with its stress on lay participation in church governance at all levels. An interpretation of the COCU proposals prepared for Presbyterians argues that the inclusion of a non-clerical perspective into the government of the church is precisely the principle behind the Presbyterian institution of ruling elders, that is, persons ecclesiastically ordained but sociologically lay.[28] Those in the Presbyterian office of ordained lay elders could be incorporated as deacons. Churches with strong episcopal traditions may ask if the bishop's authority is more than symbolic or be uncomfortable with the document's failure to differentiate the ways in which bishops and "other ministers ordained and unordained" participate in ordinations (no. 51e; cf. no. 37). Do lay people participate in the ordinations of bishops and presbyters by laying on hands? This would be contrary to the apostolic tradition.[29]

On the other hand, like the *Facing Unity* statement of the international Roman Catholic-Lutheran Joint Commission, *The COCU Consensus* suggest a way to bring previously divided churches together with a joint ministry of oversight which shares in the historic episcopate. No doubt there are some points that will have to be further refined. There is after all a provisional quality to it; it is not a constitution but points towards the future in a process of moving towards unity step by step. If it succeeds and the participating churches grow into a Church of Christ Uniting this new church will present both a formidable challenge and a new opportunity for reconciliation to the other churches.

---

[28]Lewis S. Mudge, "An Interpretation of the COCU Proposals for Presbyterians," (Atlanta and New York: Presbyterian Church U.S.A., 1986), under "What About Ruling Elders?"

[29]The theology of the Eucharist in Chapter VI of *The COCU Consensus* also needs improvement, but that is beyond our scope here.

Conclusions

We have reviewed four significant ecumenical consultations from the point of view of authority. With the caution that these statements, whether of consensus or of convergence, are for the most part the statements of theologians and still have to be received by their churches, it is still possible to suggest some indication of how authority will be understood and structured in the church of tomorow.

1. The ordained ministry is understood as one among the many gifts and ministries entrusted to the church. It cannot be understood apart from the ministry entrusted to the entire People of God, though it is a specific gift. The authority of the ordained ministry is from Christ through the Spirit. The tasks or functions of ordained ministers include preaching the word, presiding at the sacraments, and watching over the life of the church. One is authorized for this ministry by ordination with the laying on of hands, an ecclesial sign increasingly recognized as a sacramental act. Ordination to a particular ministry is not to be repeated; therefore it is permanent.

2. While there is widespread recognition that the threefold ministry of bishop, presbyter, and deacon is not the only way of structuring the church's ordained ministry, there is increasingly evident a readiness to incorporate it for the sake of unity. However both BEM and COCU stress that the threefold ministry stands in need of reform.

3. There is an emerging consensus on the importance of the episcopal office. All four consultations considered either have or are open to the office of bishop in fellowship with the historic episcopate. The episcopal succession is seen as a sign, though not a guarantee, of the continuity and unity of the church throughout the ages. What is rejected is the idea that an ordained ministry not presently in communion with the historic episcopate is not an authentic, "valid" ministry. The different churches will have to find a way to exercise the episcopal office in a collegial way with each other.

4. Though there is not yet a clear consensus on teaching authority, there is a growing recognition that the episcopal ministry includes a responsibility for guarding and teaching the apostolic faith. ARCIC sees the bishops as collectively responsible for defending the faith. The Lutheran-Catholic Dialogue in the United States acknowledges the need for Lutherans to develop structures for participating in doctrinal decision-making, while the international RC-L Joint Commission speaks of the Lutheran churches being confronted with a need to rethink teaching authority in connection with the episcopal office. Though BEM does not address the teaching authority of the bishops, *The COCU Consensus* recognizes that bishops have a responsibility for teaching both corporately and individually.

5. The exercise of authority in the church of tomorrow will hopefully be characterized by a shared responsibility. Episcopal authority will be exercised in a collegial manner. At the same time, there must be provision for a greater participation by lay people in church governance and decision-making. Certainly the process of decision-making in the church of tomorrow should involve more than the ordained. The Lutheran-Roman Catholic dialogue, BEM, and COCU speak of shared responsibility, while ARCIC implies it in its discussion of conciliarity. BEM and the RC-L statement *Facing Unity* refer to a synodal principle which provides for lay involvement. The Roman Catholic and Orthodox churches which are hierarchical in their government will have to consider ways of recognizing this synodal principle, just as some Protestant churches will have to reflect more deeply on the authority of those whose role is to oversee and preside over the preaching and sacramental life of the community.

6. Both ARCIC and the Lutheran-Roman Catholic dialogue in the United States affirm the need for a ministry of unity serving the universal church and see a reformed papal ministry as being able to fulfull this role. The international RC-L Joint Commission raises the question of a ministry to the universal unity of the church and calls for further and more detailed treatment of this question. But the difficulties

on this question should not be underestimated. For many Christians a universal authority is still contrary to their understanding of the autonomy of the local congregation.[30] BEM and COCU have not yet raised the question of the papal ministry, but certainly the question of the Petrine ministry and primacy will have to be addressed in the future.

7. Two other problems need to be considered. First, the documents considered frequently refer to the need for the "reception," both of the teaching of church authorities as well as of the ecumenical documents themselves. The question of reception is very much related to the question of authority, and needs to be considered at greater length. Second, we need to raise the question of how Christian unity might be expressed structurally. These two issues will be taken up in the remaining chapters.

[30]See, for example, C. Brownlow Hastings, "A Baptist View of Authority," in Peter J. McCord (ed.), *A Pope for All Christians?* (New York: Paulist Press, 1976), pp. 71-93.

5

Authority and Reception

So far we have concentrated on how authority is structured and exercised in the church. The concept of reception is concerned with how authoritative decisions become effective in the church's life. The term reception today is generally used in two distinct but related senses. The historical or "classical" concept refers to the acceptance by local churches of particular ecclesiastical or conciliar decisions.[1] More recently, the term has been used frequently in an ecumenical context. In this case the concept refers to the acceptance by one church of a theological consensus arrived at with another church, and ultimately, the recognition of the other church's faith and ecclesial life as authentically Christian.

In the last few years reception has become a crucial issue in this ecumenical context, for it emerges precisely at the point of the discrepancy between the progress made in the ecumenical dialogues and the apparent inability of the sponsoring churches to build and move forward on the basis of what the dialogues have accomplished. So far, none of the statements produced by the bilateral dialogues has been received by the sponsoring churches, with the exception of the Episcopal Church in the United States, which has begun the process of officially receiving the ARCIC *Final Report*. But it may be that the general frustration with the failure of the churches to officially receive the bilateral statements reflects a tendency to place too much emphasis on what formal

---

[1]John Zizioulas speaks of the "classical idea of reception" in "The Theological Problem of Reception," *Bulletin/Centro pro unione* 26 (1984) 3.

authority can accomplish by itself. Perhaps too much has been been expected of magisterial authority, as if reception were a purely juridical process. But it is much more. As Cardinal Johannes Willebrands has observed, the problem that arises in respect to the bilateral documents is "how *theological* consensuses and convergences can become *ecclesial* consensuses and convergences."[2]

The current ecumenical discussion is very much concerned with this issue. In what follows we will look at some of the past and present implications of reception. We will consider, first, the biblical roots of the concept; second, the classical and ecumenical usages of the term; third, reception as an ecclesiological reality; and finally, some suggestions for facilitating the ecumenical process of reception today.

Biblical Roots of Reception

Behind the Latin words *receptio* and *recipere* lie the New Testament Greek words *lambanein* (to receive) and *dechesthai* (to accept) and their derivatives. Paul uses the Greek equivalents for the technical rabbinic terms for the process of handing on (*paradidonai*) and receiving (*paralambanein*) the tradition. He reminds the Corinthians that they have "received" the Gospel he preached (1 Cor. 15:1); similarly, he tells them that they have received the Holy Spirit (1 Cor. 1:12). In the parable of the seed the word is accepted (Mk. 4:20); in Acts Peter's preaching is accepted by those who are subsequently baptized (Acts 2:41). Those who accept Jesus and his messengers in doing so also accept God (*dechesthai*, Matt. 10:40; *lambanein* Jn. 13:20).

What resulted from the reception of the apostolic preaching by those who became the converts of the apostles and other early Christian missionaries was the church itself. The same dynamic can be seen in the formation of the New Testament canon.[3] Those Christian writings which were ac-

[2]Cardinal Johannes Willebrands, "The Ecumenical Dialogue and Its Reception," *Bulletin/Centro pro unione* 27 (1985) 6.

[3]Ulrich Kuhn, "Reception—An Imperative and an Opportunity," in *Ecumenical*

cepted by the early communities as expressions of the apostolic faith became through this process of reception part of the church's canon of Sacred Scripture. Still later the receiving of liturgical practices, church laws, and customs of one church by others further illustrates the process of reception. As examples, Edward Kilmartin points to the fourth century reception of the Spirit *epiklesis* in the East, to the acceptance of the Roman liturgy in Germany beginning in the sixth century, and to the reception of the Mainz Pontifical by Rome in the tenth.[4]

Reception: Classical and Ecumenical

1. *The Classical Concept.* Although reception as an ecclesiological reality has a broad application, the term in its classical sense is used restrictively to refer to the acceptance in the early church of conciliar decrees and decisions, particularly those of the great ecumenical councils. Ulrich Kuhn points out that those writing in the last twenty years tend to speak of reception in the ancient church in two main connections. First, in the pre-Constantinian period reception is primarily concerned with the process through which decisions of local or regional synods were made known to and accepted by other churches. Kuhn stresses that what underlies this practice is the recognition that a particular church is authentically church only if it lives in communion with other churches.[5]

Secondly, since the time of Constantine, the focus has been generally on the process through which those decisions made by the great "ecumenical" councils were discussed, interpreted, and received by local churches or a later council.[6] An example would be the acceptance of the doctrinal decrees

Perspectives on Baptism, Eucharist and Ministry, ed. Max Thurian (Geneva: WCC, 1983), p. 166.

[4]Edward J. Kilmartin, "Reception in History: An Ecclesiological Phenomenon and Its Significance," *Journal of Ecumenical Studies* 21 (1984) 41-43.

[5]Kuhn, "Reception," p. 166.

[6]Ibid., p. 167.

of the Council of Nicaea (325), though only after considerable opposition. Other examples include that of Pope Leo II, who both confirmed the teachings of Constantinople III (681) and asked the Spanish bishops to support it with their own authority, which they did at the regional Council of Toledo XIV (684).[7]

But the process might also lead to a rejection. The church ultimately did not receive the claim of Boniface VIII in the bull *Unam Sanctam* (1302) "that it is absolutely necessary for the salvation of all men that they submit to the Roman pontiff" (DS 875). Similarly, the conciliarist teaching on the supremacy of a general assembly of bishops over a pope expressed in the decree *Haec Sancta* (1415) of the Council of Constance was not received by the church, though the validity and intention of this decree still provokes debate among theologians.

The classical concept of reception must be understood as an ecclesiological reality which emerged in the life of the church of the first millennium. It is most important to note that during this period the church was understood as a communion of churches. It is this ecclesiology of communion as well as the practice which it grounded which have important implications for the church of today. The concept of reception was still implicit in the ecclesiology of the canonists of the twelfth and thirteen centuries.[8] But the excessively hierarchical concept of church which developed in the late medieval and post-Tridentine church tends to reduce reception to a purely juridical category,[9] if indeed it does not so emphasize the role of ecclesiastical authority that the notion of reception is virtually rejected.[10]

[7]Kilmartin, "Reception in History," p. 49.

[8]See Brian Tierney, "'Only the Truth Has Authority': The Problem of 'Reception' in the Decretists and in Johannes de Turrecremate," in *Law, Church and Society: Essays in Honor of Stephan Kuttner*, ed. Kenneth Pennington and Robert Somerville (University of Pennsylvania Press, 1977), pp. 69-96.

[9]Kilmartin, "Reception in History," pp. 35-36.

[10]Yves Congar, "Reception as an Ecclesiological Reality," in *Election and Consensus in the Church*, ed. Guiseppe Alberigo and Anton Weiler (Concilium 77) (New York: Herder and Herder, 1972), p. 60.

If the ecclesiology which developed in the later part of the second millennium was excessively hierarchical, that does not mean that reception as a reality in the praxis of the church had entirely disappeared. A recent study of the papacy by J. Robert Dionne demonstrates how the teachings of the ordinary papal magisterium beginning with Pius IX and continued by his successors were modified or reversed by the Second Vatican Council as a result of theologians "talking back" to Rome.[11] Among them Dionne includes Pius IX's position denying the presence of any truth or goodness in non-Christian religions, his condemnation of the proposition that there should be a separation of church and state, along with the correlative question of religious freedom as an objective right, and Piux XII's exclusive identification of the Roman Catholic Church with the Mystical Body of Christ. These papal teachings ultimately were modified or reversed because of what he calls the "modalities" of their reception.

2. *The Ecumenical Concept.* While the classical concept emerged in a church which understood itself as a communion of churches, it was nonetheless a united church. In the ecumenical context, however, a new element appears, for now what is involved is a process of reception between churches separated from one another by differences of history, doctrine, and structure. In the absence of communion between the churches, the process of reception is complicated considerably. As Anton Houtepen observes, "More theological consensus is needed to restore unity than to preserve unity."[12]

From the time of its founding in 1948, the World Council of Churches has been working to build consensus among the churches, receiving reports and statements and forwarding them to its member churches "for their study and appropriate action."[13] So the ecumenical process of reception has already been initiated.

[11]J. Robert Dionne, *The Papacy and the Church: A Study of Praxis and Reception in Ecumenical Perspective*, (New York: Philosophical Library, 1987).

[12]Anton Houtepen, "Reception, Tradition, Communion," in Thurian, *Ecumenical Perspectives*, p. 148.

[13]See "The Rules of the World Council of Churches" XIV, 6, (a) in *Breaking Barriers: Nairobi 1975*, ed. David M. Paton (London: SPCK, 1976), p. 339.

As a formal, ecumenical concept, reception first began to emerge as a result of a meeting on the ancient councils organized by the Faith and Order Commission at Oxford in 1965 and then at Bad Gastein, Austria, in 1966.[14] Gradually both the concept and the term became part of the ecumenical vocabulary. Zizioulas mentions an attempt to use the concept of reception in a decisive way at the Faith and Order meeting at Louvain in 1972.[15] The WCC statement *One Baptism, One Eucharist and a Mutually Recognized Ministry* approved at Accra in 1974 did not speak specifically of reception, but it was "submitted to the churches for consideration and comment."[16] The WCC Assembly at Nairobi in 1975 specifically called the churches "to receive, reappropriate and confess together . . . the Christian truth and faith, delivered through the Apostles and handed down through the centuries."[17] And when the WCC text *Baptism, Eucharist and Ministry* (BEM) was published and transmitted to the churches throughout the world in 1982, the Faith and Order Commission invited all the churches "to prepare an official response . . . at the highest appropriate level of authority" as part of "this process of reception."[18]

Thus the ecumenical movement and, especially since the end of the Second Vatican Council, the appearance of the various bilateral dialogues, along with the official statements formulated by them, have made the issue of reception unavoidable.

Reception as an Ecclesiological Reality

We have reviewed the classical and ecumenical concepts of reception. If both are understood in the context of the broader ecclesiological reality of reception of which each

[14]Zizioulas, "The Theological Problem," p. 3.

[15]Ibid.

[16]*One Baptism, One Eucharist and a Mutually Recognized Ministry* (Geneva: WCC, 1975), p. 5.

[17]*Breaking Barriers: Nairobi, 1975*, Report of Section II, p. 66.

[18]*Baptism, Eucharist and Ministry* (Geneva: WCC, 1982), p.x.

remains a part, a number of conclusions can be drawn.

1. Reception cannot be reduced to a juridical determination, either of authority or on the part of the faithful; it is a process involving the whole church. In the ancient church ecclesiastical decisions or teachings became normative for the later church only when they were received by the communion of churches and ultimately by the faithful themselves. At the same time, reception does not constitute a decision as legitimate. Congar emphasizes that reception "does not confer validity, but affirms, acknowledges and attests that this matter is for the good of the Church."[19] In other words, reception guarantees that a decision or teaching will be efficacious in the life of the church.

Vatican II teaches that the whole church is involved in grasping Christian truth.

> The body of the faithful as a whole, anointed as they are by the Holy One (cf. 1 Jn. 2:20, 27), cannot err in matters of belief. Thanks to a supernatural sense of the faith which characterizes the People as a whole, it manifests this unerring quality when, 'from the bishops down to the last member of the laity,' it shows universal agreement in matters of faith and morals.[20]

More recently, Cardinal Willebrands has stressed that reception cannot be understood "as a purely technical or instrumental concept"; he argues that it involves the whole People of God and in this sense "has certain aspects of a sociological process."[21] Thus it involves the research activities of theologians, "the preserving fidelity and piety" of the faithful, and the binding decisions arrived at by the college of bishops.[22]

As a contemporary example of reception, Willebrands

---

[19]Congar, "Reception," p. 66.

[20]*Dogmatic Constitution on the Church* (LG), no. 12 in *The Documents of Vatican II*, ed. Walter M. Abbott (New York: the America Press, 1966), p.29.

[21]Willebrands, "The Ecumenical Dialogue," p. 5.

[22]Ibid., p. 6.

points to the reception of the ecumenical movement itself by Vatican II, a reception made possible by earlier developments in theology, in the Christian lives of the faithful, and in some "often hesitant" statements of the magisterium.[23] At the same time, not all initiatives on the part of authority have been received by the faithful. John Long calls attention to the failure of church authorities in the fifteenth century to translate the agreements between the eastern churches and the Latin west reached at the Council of Florence into terms intelligible to the clergy and faithful of both traditions, with the sad result that this attempt at reconciliation itself failed.[24] Congar points to Pope John XXIII's apostolic constitution *Veterum sapientia*, recommending the continuation of the use of Latin especially in seminaries, as an example of church legislation not received by the faithful.[25] The question could also be raised as to whether or not *Humanae vitae*, Pope Paul VI's encyclical on artificial contraception, has been genuinely received by the faithful.[26]

2. Reception also involves formal decisions on the part of church authorities. In the classical model of reception the bishop symbolized the link between the local church and the apostolic church; the bishop also maintained the communion between the local church and the universal church by participating in conciliar gatherings.[27] Sometimes it was the role of the bishops in council to initiate a process of reception through formal conciliar decisions. The creed proclaimed by the Council of Nicaea (325) is an obvious example. For a council itself to be ecumenical, it must be received by the Bishop of Rome.[28] Sometimes the authority of the bishops served to give formal approval to a process of reception

---

[23]Ibid., p. 5.

[24]John Long, "Reception: Ecumenical Dialogue at a Turning Point," *Ecumenical Trends* 12 (1983) 19-20. Long refers to Joseph Gill's study, *The Council of Florence* (Cambridge: University Press, 1959).

[25]Congar, "Reception," p. 57.

[26]See Joseph A. Komonchak, "*Humanae vitae* and Its Reception: Ecclesiological Reflections," *Theological Studies* 39 (1978) 221-57.

[27]Zizioulas, "The Theological Problem," p. 5.

[28]Congar, "Reception," p. 51.

already underway, thus bringing the process to a juridical close. For example, the practice of private, frequent confession, brought to the European Continent by the Irish missionaries in the sixth and seventh centuries, was only gradually received there. Yet it finally became the official and universal practice when the Fourth Lateran Council (1215) decreed that every Christian who committed a serious sin should confess it within a year.

Therefore church authorities have a role to play in the process of reception, but they do not carry out that role simply by making juridical decisions. Their role is to articulate what is the faith of the church. Even the dogma of infallibility is essentially a statement about the church, not about the pope, or the pope and the bishops, apart from the church. The statement in the constitution *Pastor aeternus* at Vatican I that solemn definitions of the pope are "irreformable of themselves [*ex sese*], and not from the consent of the Church,"[29] means only that papal teachings are not dependent on subsequent juridical approval by national hierarchies, as the Gallican view maintained. In saying that "the Roman Pontiff ... is possessed of that infallibility with which the Divine Redeemer willed that his Church should be endowed," the Council was pointing to how the church's infallibility comes to expression.[30] Vatican II clarified the teaching of Vatican I by including the college of bishops in the exercise of the church's charism of infallibility, at the same time pointing out that to "the resulting definitions the assent of the Church can never be wanting, on account of the activity of that same Holy Spirit, whereby the whole flock of Christ is preserved and progresses in unity of faith."[31]

3. Reception cannot be reduced to the acceptance of doctrinal formulations; it involves the recognition and acceptance of a common faith. Forms of worship, life, and practice emerge out of a living tradition which bears the faith experience of a community. To accept a liturgical practice from

[29]DS 3074.
[30]Ibid.
[31]LG no. 25, Abbott p. 49.

another community is to acknowledge a shared faith which comes to expression through a ritual.

The same holds true for doctrinal formulations. When the representatives of churches in dialogue are able to arrive at a statement of consensus or agreement on those issues which have previously divided them, the completion of the dialogue process represents more than the mutual acceptance of a linguistic formula; it also implies the recognition of a common faith. That common faith is often expressed differently in the various Christians traditions, and no particular expression, no matter how true, completely captures the reality with which it is concerned. There will always be a diversity of expression.[32] But when a consensus based on a common language is reached, the dialogue partners are beginning to discover each other as sharing the same faith.

The process of reception has already begun when two churches, in spite of their separate histories, commit themselves to the search for unity by entering into dialogue. Such a commitment implies not just a willingness to trust each other, but also the recognition of the dialogue partner as a community of Christians also living a Christian life. Furthermore, entering into dialogue commits each church to re-examine its own tradition and ecclesial life in the light of Scripture and the dialogue itself.[33]

4. The norm for recognizing a common faith is not agreement with one's own ecclesial position but agreement with the apostolic tradition. In his study of reception Edward Kilmartin singles out the work of Herman Josef Sieben as the best description of the relationship between reception and the authority of ecumenical councils, formulated as a *consensio antiquitatis et universitatis* which is grounded in the work of the Holy Spirit.[34] The *consensio universitatis* represented the "horizontal consensus" of the whole church

---

[32]Cf. Robert Butterworth, "Reception and Pluriformity," *Month* 18 (1985) 348-58.

[33]Kuhn, "Reception," p. 169.

[34]Kilmartin, "Reception in History," 48-50; see Herman Josef Sieben, *Die Konzilsidee der alten Kirche* (Paderborn: Schöningh, 1979) 511-16.

which the council had to express and which had to be secured by reception. But the *consensio antiquitatis*, the "vertical consensus" with the teaching of Scripture and the apostolic tradition, had to be demonstrated by the council and tested by the whole church. Of the two, Kilmartin argues, the vertical consensus, which includes the element of formal authority, has priority and "is ultimately decisive because the truth of faith is, from its essence, a truth handed on."[35] In other words, in receiving the teaching of a council an individual church was acknowledging that its own life of faith received from the apostolic tradition could be expressed by the conciliar decision.

J. M. R. Tillard also stresses the apostolic tradition as norm. He warns against making the term reception so extensive that it loses any specific meaning. The correct approach in respect to any ecumenical accord must be found "in subjecting it to a critical evaluation in the light of the apostolic tradition," for the essential requirement is not merely mutual understanding but rather "a collective conversion to the claims of the apostolic faith *as such*."[36]

Tillard suggests several practical considerations for those willing to implement reception with the conversion it implies. First, they should beware of accepting only what is already included in their own tradition. Second, there must be a willingness to inquire if an ecclesial element present in another tradition and absent from one's own—even if one's own tradition dates from the earliest Christian centuries—is not a deficiency.[37] Finally, in the case of one tradition lacking something strongly present in another, the question must be asked: "Does this lack arise from a denial of the point at issue, or from an alternative and valid interpretation which also has its roots in the great apostolic tradition?"[38]

---

[35]Ibid. pp. 146-47.

[36]J.M.R. Tillard, "'Reception': A Time to Beware of False Steps," *Ecumenical Trends* 14 (1985) 145; Tillard's emphasis.

[37]Ibid., pp. 146-47.

[38]Ibid., p. 148.

Reception Today

Agreed statements formulated by theologians are important steps on the road to a future communion between the sponsoring churches. But the statements by themselves will not be able to bring the churches together. Reception, especially in an ecumenical context, must involve the whole church. That means a recognition on the part of whole communities hitherto estranged from one another that they share a common faith and a common ecclesial life. Hence it involves a change of perception.

When churches have been separated from each other by differences of doctrine, structure, and spirituality; when they do not have a common history, they must rediscover some shared Christian experience if the reception of agreed statements is to be complete and ultimately lead to reconciliation. What is needed is a new "intersubjective reality" which can help Christians from different communities to recognize each other as sharing the same faith. Without this discovery and therefore the recognition of each other as sisters and brothers in the Lord, the process of reception, already well begun, will fizzle out.

Anyone who has been involved in ecumenism usually has a personal story which contributes to the process of discovery. Each one will tell how his or her perception of other Christians and traditions has changed through personal contact and a deepening relationship with the other. Roman Catholics marvel at the reverence with which other Christians celebrate the Eucharist. Protestants are touched to discover the place the Bible holds in the personal prayer and spirituality of many Catholics. Pentecostals have been surprised to discover the flourishing of spiritual gifts among charismatic Roman Catholics and mainline Protestants.

Professional ecumenists tend to forget how unfamiliar many Christians are with the faith and ecclesial life of Christians from other traditions. If the different churches are ever to receive the considerable consensus which has already been achieved on a theological level, their members must begin to experience each other's faith experience as their own. Then they will begin to experience communion. How can this process of reception be facilitated today?

1. On an educational level, the results of the dialogues must enter into the practical life of the churches. Liturgies should incorporate the consensus emerging on baptism and Eucharist. As Lukas Vischer has pointed out, a particular tradition might have to reconsider the importance of the eucharistic epiklesis; another might have to express more clearly the importance of personal belief in baptism. Catechisms should be updated to include the agreement reached through the dialogues.[39]

2. The most effective way for Christians from different traditions to discover a common faith is through living and worshipping together. The Third World Conference on Faith and Order (Lund, 1952) proposed as a principle that the churches "act together in all matters except those in which deep differences of conviction compel them to act separately."[40] More recently, in responding to the *Final Report*, the Catholic bishops of England and Wales have made a similar affirmation:

> We wish to endorse, in particular, the spirit of the last sentence of the *Final Report*: 'We suggest that some difficulties will not be wholly resolved until a practical initiative has been taken and our two Churches have lived together more visibly in one *koinonia*.' It is widespread experience of many people in our countries that the work of ecumenism must be carried out at all levels and in all dimensions of Church life. Doctrinal discussions alone are not sufficient.[41]

Those who have lived in ecumenical communities have experienced the power of common worship, though not without cost, especially when intercommunion is the issue. Des-

---

[39]Lukas Vischer, "The Process of 'Reception' in the Ecumenical Movement," *Mid-Stream* 23 (1984) 231.

[40]*The Third World Conference on Faith and Order, August 15-28, 1952*, ed. Oliver Tomkins (London: SCM, 1953), p. 16.

[41]*One in Christ* 21 (1985) 179-80.

pite the pain of not being able to share the Eucharist, Christians from five or six different church traditions in the l'Arche communities of England and Scotland live, work, and pray together. Taizé in France has helped the whole church to rediscover a common language of liturgical prayer. Grandchamp in Switzerland and Iona in Scotland have given many a new sense of a common faith and awakened in them a desire for Christian unity. Those in ecumenical "covenant" communities within the charismatic renewal have experienced something similar. Thus ecumenical communities have an important role to play in helping Christians of different traditions discover how much they share in common. Churches and congregations can move in this direction by using a common lectionary, taking advantage of opportunities for common prayer, and increasing the ecumenical character of their preaching.

Yet too often the very thought of Christians from different traditions living and worshipping together is resisted precisely because of the issue of intercommunion. If, however, it is true that reception involves not just church authorities but the entire People of God, the question must be raised as to what it means when Christians from different traditions— Roman Catholics among them—are able to recognize the Lord's presence in one another's celebrations of the Eucharist, even though their church leaders have yet to acknowledge this. Is it not simply a fact that many Christians today would not raise questions about the "validity" of eucharistic celebrations in other churches unless the traditional difficulties were pointed out to them? Local church authorities should consider and weigh carefully the experience of their people, not as an instance of the collapse of discipline, but as part of the process of reception already underway. There has been some progress in this area; interim sharing of the Eucharist has been authorized for Episcopalians and some Lutherans on the basis of the dialogue between the Episcopal Church in the United States and the three Lutheran churches now reorganized as the new Evangelical Lutheran Church of America.

3. Short of intercommunion—which presupposes an experienced koinonia—there are many opportunities for joint ministry. The Catholic Worker communities across the United States and the Sojourner community in the nation's capital have been particularly effective in bringing together Christians of different traditions in a common social ministry nourished by prayer and community life. Over the last twenty years many Christians working together for social justice have found a new communion which cuts across denominational lines.

There are many areas in which local parishes and congregations can begin to co-operate by pooling their resources. Before talking about common worship, common schools, or common plants, neighboring parishes might at least consider a joint vacation Bible school or social-outreach program. Many are already working together to assist the homeless, refugees, and the elderly. These efforts also assist Christians from different traditions to discover the extent to which they share the same faith, and so helps in the process of reception.

4. Local churches should themselves enter into the reception process. An important precedent was set for the Roman Catholic Church when, thanks to the Secretariat for the Promoting of Christian Unity, the process of responding to BEM and the *Final Report* was broadened beyond the church's central administration in Rome so that national episcopal conferences and ultimately local churches could also take part. Thus local Catholic churches throughout the world (or English-speaking churches in the case of the *Final Report*) for the first time are able to become involved in the process of reception. As of June 1986 in the United States, out of some 180 dioceses and archdioceses, only 21 had submitted reactions to BEM and eight to the *Final Report*. Certainly not an overwhelming response.

Often the objection is raised that the resources are lacking; the local church does not have the experts, theologians, seminaries, or institutes needed to formulate a response to an ecumenical text such as BEM or the *Final Report*. But that is to leave ecumenism in the hands of the specialists and runs the risk of reducing reception to the acceptance of doctrinal formulations. Local churches need to develop their own ways of responding, using the resources and structures available. A first step might be to conduct a series of hearings, listening to those involved in ecumenical encounters at university campus ministry centers, retreat houses, ecumenical communities, the various renewal movements, and other activities in which Christians from different churches are engaged. The hearings conducted recently by the Catholic Church in the United States on the issue of women in the church could serve as a model. Ecumenical groups might reflect together on an agreed statement during a particular liturgical season such as Lent or Advent or at a weekend retreat. The local ecumenical commission could prepare a written response incorporating the experience of people in the local church as well as theological reflection on the document itself.

5. Finally, churches at the national or regional level should begin to respond to ecumenical initiatives in a way that goes beyond offering theological reactions to dialogue statements. One hopeful sign for such a step forward appears at the end of the National Conference of Catholic Bishops' evaluation of the *Final Report* in what appears to be a recommendation for a joint synod of Roman Catholic and Anglican bishops. The NCCB evaluation concludes: "Looking ahead to the future, we hope that ARCIC II will be asked to prepare its conclusions for a session of the Synod of Bishops with Anglican input *and representation*."[42]

Conclusions

It is unfortunate that today more energy seems to go into the preservation of confessional or doctrinal identity than into building on the ecumenical progress that has already been achieved. The ecumenical dialogues have displayed substantial areas of agreement. They need to be received, but

[42]"Evaluation of the Final Report," *Ecumenical Trends* 14 (1985) 23; emphasis mine.

this demands more than a juridical decision on the part of church authorities. If the classical concept of reception presumed an ecclesiology of communion, then it is essential today that local and regional churches themselves become involved in the reception process. When separated Christians experience each other's faith as their own and when they recognize in each other the Lord's presence, then they will take the steps necessary to express their communion.

6

Imaging Tomorrow's Church: Models of Christian Unity

A few years ago Heinrich Fries and Karl Rahner jointly authored a little book with the provocative title, *Unity of the Churches: A Real Possibility.*[1] Intended to address the resignation and discouragement experienced by many in the ecumenical movement, the two theologians rejected the view that the friendlier relationships which had developed between the churches in recent years represented the best that could be hoped for at the present time. Given the present state of theology, they argued, the unity of the churches is actually possible today; the conditions and presuppositions necessary to bring it about are already present in the churches themselves. Their book spells out those conditions and presuppositions in eight theses, ranging from the doctrinal parameters of unity to the acceptance and exercise of the Petrine office.

Not all were happy with the book. Bishop Peter L'Huillier, Orthodox bishop of the Diocese of New York, described the approach as "unrealistic."[2] Father Daniel Ols, a French theologian reported in a number of magazines as representing the Vatican point of view, accused the authors of trying to

[1]Heinrich Fries and Karl Rahner, *Unity of the Churches: A Real Possibility,* trans. Ruth C.L. Gritsch and Eric Gritsch (New York/Philadelphia: Paulist Press/Fortress Press, 1985).

[2]Peter L'Huillier, "An Orthodox Response," *Ecumenical Trends* 14 (July/August 1985) 101.

take some "ecumenical short-cuts."[3] Cardinal Joseph Ratzinger, head of the Vatican's Congregation for the Doctrine
of the Faith, characterized it as "theological acrobatics"
(*theologische Akrobatik*).[4] No doubt there were flaws in the
plan for unity which Fries and Rahner offered. It certainly
could be refined. But what was perhaps most significant
about their book was that it represented an attempt to
imagine concretely how unity among the churches might be
realized. In making this effort, they have performed a sing-
ular service, for the issue of how the church of tomorrow
might combine a catholic fullness and universality with an
ecumenical inclusiveness of particular churches and traditions
needs to be addressed.

The difficulty about envisioning the church unity that so
many desire does not come from a lack of imagination—
since imagination is always at work, consciously or on a
subliminal level. There are a number of different images of
unity present in the Christian community today, though these
images have not always been clearly grasped and developed.
The difficulty comes from a lack of realism about the kind of
unity that is possible or even desirable. In what follows we
will consider four different models of unity: organic union,
conciliar fellowship, reconciled diversity, and communion of
churches. The models to be considered here are neither new
nor exhaustive of the possibilities.[5] But to the extent that
they are specific they can help clarify our thinking and perhaps free us to face the future with both realism and hope.

[3]Daniel Ols, "Scorciatoie ecumeniche," *L'Osservatore Romano* 47 (Feb. 25-26,
1985).

[4]Reported in *Herder Korrespondenz*, "Ruckkehrökumene," 38 (January 1984) 4.

[5]See for example Günter Gassmann and Harding Meyer, *The Unity of the
Church: Requirements and Structure* (Geneva: Lutheran World Federation, 1983);
Yves Congar, *Diversity and Communion* (Mystic, Connecticut: Twenty-Third
Publications, 1984); also William G. Rusch, *Ecumenism: A Movement Toward
Church Unity* (Philadelphia: Fortress Press, 1985), pp. 118-22; five models of union
are described in the Roman Catholic-Lutheran International Commission document
entitled *Facing Unity: Models, Forms and Phases of Catholic-Lutheran Fellowship*
(LWF, 1985), pp. 12-17.

Organic Union

The organic union model—sometimes referred to as corporate union—envisions Christian unity as involving a single, united institution. Until very recent times most Roman Catholics thought of Christian unity exclusively in terms of this model. A schema for the Constitution on the Church of Christ, prepared for but never voted on by the bishops assembled at Vatican Council I (1870) described the church as a hierarchized "perfect society" with a visible and undivided unity.[6] From this perspective, ecumenism meant that those separated from the "true" church would give up the errors of their ways and their separate ecclesial traditions and "return to Rome." This view found considerable support in official Roman documents. In 1928, not long after the first Faith and Order Conference at Lausanne, Pope Pius XI issued the encyclical *Mortalium Animos*, forbidding the participation of Roman Catholics in the ecumenical assemblies of non-Catholics. The pope was quite clear about how Christian unity was to be achieved: "There is only one way in which the unity of Christians may be fostered, and that is by promoting the return to the one true Church of Christ of those who are separated from it; for from that one true Church they have in the past unhappily fallen away."[7]

Some Protestant commentators, speaking nostalgically of the sixteenth century Lutheran reformers' original vision of reform within the universal church, have helped perpetuate the organic union model. Both George Lindbeck and Carl Braaten have used the image of Protestants as exiles, driven from their homeland in the one church by a usurping tyrannical government and forced to set up a new government or ecclesial order in exile.[8]

---

[6]See *The First Draft of the Constitution on the Church of Christ* in *The Teaching of the Catholic Church*, ed. Karl Rahner, orginially prepared by Josef Neuner and Heinrich Roos (Staten Island, New York: Alba House, 1967), pp. 213-15.

[7]*Acta Apostolicae Sedis* 20 (1928) 5-15, p. 14.

[8]See George A. Lindbeck, "A Protestant View of the Ecclesiological Status of the Roman Catholic Church," *Journal of Ecumenical Studies, Studies,* 1 (1964) 244-46; Carl E. Braaten, "The Reunited Church of the Future," *Journal of Ecumenical Studies,* 4 (1967) 611-28.

There is much truth in this image or parable, though it should not be understood as advocating a simplistic return to Rome. Protestant Christians value their own ecclesial traditions and their independence which they understand as an expression of Christian freedom rooted in the Gospel. They are not interested in a monolithic super-church. At the same time the image serves to underline that the current situation of a Christianity divided into separate churches cannot be accepted as anything more than a provisional solution to a problem not yet resolved. No church is self-sufficient; it needs to be in communion with other churches.

Furthermore, it illustrates that organic union cannot be understood as a merger in which each church might give up what other churches hold as unacceptable; such a "lowest common denominator" ecumenism would also be inadequate. As Lindbeck pointed out in 1964, speaking of apostolic succession through the episcopal office, the Orthodox and Roman Catholic churches have something which the Protestant churches lack; "they have visible institutional continuity with the early church."[9] In Braaten's interpretation of the image, the reunited church of the future will need to include papal and episcopal structures as well as apostolic succession, though papacy and episcopacy will be acceptable to Protestants only when they have been divested of every feature of authoritarianism, both in theory and in practice.[10]

Therefore the inadequacy of the organic union model does not rule out the need to find a way to incorporate Catholic structures such as episcopacy and the Petrine ministry into tomorrow's church.

Conciliar Fellowship

The Fifth Assembly of the World Council of Churches, held at Nairobi from November 23 to December 10, 1975, developed a vision of Christian unity as a conciliar fellowship. The crucial sentence from the Assembly reads as fol-

[9]Lindbeck, p. 251.
[10]Braaten, p. 618.

lows: "The one church is to be envisioned as a conciliar fellowship of local churches which are themselves truly united."[11] Though this model has sometimes been understood in terms of a conciliar assembly of national churches, thus as an assembly such as the World Council itself represents, this is not what the Nairobi Assembly had in mind. The Nairobi statement specifically pointed out that the "present inter-confessional assemblies are not councils in this full sense, because they are not yet united by a common understanding of the apostolic faith, by common ministry, and a common Eucharist."[12]

The key term in the phrase "conciliar fellowship of local churches" is "local." A report from the 1974 meeting of the Faith and Order Commission at Accra, Ghana, acknowledged that full and effective unity at the local level could be referred to as organic union; more specifically, it made clear that unity at the local level would lead the church beyond the problem of overlapping jurisdictions, the situation where "two different bishops or committees both claim a similar authority for the same place or sector of the common life."[13] Thus the model of conciliar fellowship, at least as it has been developed by the WCC, rules out the co-existence of several independent churches in the same locality.

An example of this model of church unity is provided by some of the "united" churches. A number of these transconfessional unions have appeared in recent years, among them the United Church of Canada (1925) and the Uniting Church in Australia (1977), both of which join Congregationalists, Methodists, and Presbyterians. One of the most interesting examples, the Church of South India, unites Congregationalists, Presbyterians, Methodists, and Anglicans in a single church which has incorporated the historic episcopate, received from the Anglicans. This new church, established in 1947, recognized the ministries of the pastors from each of

---

[11] *Breaking Barriers: Nairobi 1975*, ed. David M. Paton (London: SPCK, 1976) Section II, p. 60.

[12] Ibid., p. 61

[13] "The Unity of the Church: the Goal and the Way,"in *Uniting in Hope: Accra 1974* (Geneva: WCC, 1975), p. 118.

the uniting churches while requiring that future ministers receive the laying on of hands from a bishop, to preserve the apostolic succession. The Church of North India (1970) includes these traditions as well as Baptists and Brethren. Both of these churches have been included within the wider Anglican Fellowship associated with the worldwide Anglican Communion; though not actually members of the communion, their members may receive the Eucharist in Anglican churches but their ordained ministers must be "licensed" by the local bishop in order to function within one.

The model of conciliar fellowship, with its vision of a united local church which would include various traditions, is attractive. Certainly the various united churches have an important role to play on the journey towards unity, and there must must be a place for them in the church of tomorrow.

But there are a number of problems with the conciliar fellowship model. First, since it envisions a future church as a community of local churches, for the Roman Catholic Church to participate it would have to give up its character as a worldwide church with a universal teaching authority and jurisdiction and transform itself into a federation of independent local or regional churches. In a sense this would be to suggest that the Catholic Church give up what it regards as its catholicity. Thus the problem of how to reconcile a universal communion with the independence of local churches remains unresolved.

Second, representatives of confessional traditions such as the Lutheran and the Reformed frequently object to the model on the grounds that it presupposes a transcending or suppressing of confessional identities on the local level. They find this anti-confessional approach unacceptable.[14]

[14]See for example "Harding Meyer on the Idea of 'Reconciled Diversity'," in Congar, *Diversity and Communion*, p. 154.

Reconciled Diversity

The model favored by the confessional churches is termed "reconciled diversity." It was recommended in a *Working Paper on the Ecumenical Role of World Confessional Alliances* developed in 1974 for the Conference of Secretaries of World Confessional Alliances.[15] In 1977 the Lutheran World Federation adopted a proposal of reconciled diversity at its assembly at Dar-es-Salaam.[16] Reconciled diversity looks to an ecumenical community of churches which maintain their own confessional identities and structures while reestablishing communion in preaching, eucharistic sharing, ministry, and service.

Using the World Council of Churches as a model, Oscar Cullmann suggests a council which could unite the various churches while allowing them to preserve their diversity in structure and government.[17] Though not itself a church, such a council could provide a superstructure for the member churches which could deliberate and make decisions, as long as these decisions did not infringe upon those made by the various member churches through their own synods or councils.[18] Thus his model combines aspects of conciliar fellowship and reconciled diversity.

What is to be said for the model of reconciled diversity? Does it represent a solution to the problem of a divided Christianity by the simple procedure of declaring past differences resolved and then restoring communion between communities which will continue to live as separate churches? One proponent, the Strasbourg ecumenist Harding Meyer, argues that reconciled diversity does not merely sanction the *status quo*. He insists that it involves not a smoothing over of confessional differences but a process of change and renewal through dialogue which would eliminate elements

[15]Ibid., pp. 155-56.

[16]Congar, *Diversity and Communion*, p. 149. See *In Christ—A New Community*, The Proceedings of the Sixth Assembly of the Lutheran World Federation, Dar-es-Salaam 1977 (Geneva: LWF, 1977).

[17]Oscar Cullmann, *Unity through Diversity* (Philadelphia: Fortress Press, 1988).

[18]Ibid., pp. 60-64.

which have disfigured and distorted the confessional traditions and redefine the diversities in the different churches in a way which would affirm their legitimacy.[19]

But questions remain. Would the concept of a reconciled diversity provide sufficient doctrinal consensus and the structures of unity necessary to support a common ecclesial life and mission, or would it represent no more than an apparent reconciliation? Would Cullman's council, with its limited authority, really allow the community of churches to address significant issues with one voice? The French Dominican Yves Congar finds a problem with the fact that the proposal for unity based on a reconciled diversity starts from the situation of the existing divisions rather from the reality of the undivided church with its unity flowing from its inner life.[20]

Communion of Churches

Since the Second Vatican Council, with its emphasis on collegiality, the concept of communion (*koinonia*) has moved to the center of Roman Catholic ecclesiology. The report of the 1985 Extraordinary Synod of Bishops states that the Roman Catholic Church has fully assumed its ecumenical responsibility on the basis of the ecclesiology of communion.[21] Thus Roman Catholic ecumenical theology sees the future union of Christians in terms of this model.

An ecclesiology of communion recalls the way in which the church of the first millennium understood itself and functioned; the church "catholic" was constituted by a communion of churches. The New Testament word *koinonia*, often translated as fellowship, has the sense of a participation or sharing in something else. It is first used in the New Testament by St. Paul to designate the relationship which exists between the believer and the Lord (1 Cor. 1:9), and

---

[19]Meyer in Congar, *Diversity and Communion*, p. 157.

[20]Congar, pp. 151-152.

[21]Extraordinary Synod of Bishops, Rome, 1985, published as *A Message to the People of God and the Final Report* (Washington: USCC, 1986), pp. 20-21.

consequently, the relationship which unites the believers among themselves. At the root of Paul's vision of the unity of the church is the Eucharist, for through their *koinonia* in the body and blood of Christ, the believers themselves become one body (1 Cor. 10:16-17).

In the post-New Testament church the word *koinonia* or communion came to be used in conjunction with those sacramental and institutional elements through which the unity of the church as a visible, social, and ultimately worldwide community was expressed. Thus the concept of communion, whether it refers to the relation of the individual to the church community or the relation that churches have among themselves, describes a real, social relationship, and therefore a relationship which has a visible, public, or even institutional character. The link between the local church and the universal church has been symbolized and expressed historically by the bishops who represent the local churches both in the ordination of bishops during a eucharistic celebration and in conciliar gatherings.

The concept of the one church as a communion of churches is, of course, familiar to the Orthodox. Both the Roman Catholic Church and the Orthodox churches understand each other as sharing a common faith, common sacraments, and a common apostolic heritage. In their best moments, the two churches have spoken of each other as "sister" churches. At Vatican II the Roman Catholic Church reaffirmed the right of the churches of the East to govern themselves according to their own disciplines.[22] And the East, though it does not accept a primacy such as was defined by the First Vatican Council, is willing to recognize the Church of Rome as enjoying a primacy of honor among churches equal in dignity.

Bracketing for the moment the question of primacy, a renewed understanding of the church as a communion of churches offers the best possibility for a reintegration of the Orthodox churches and the Roman Catholic Church in a single fellowship. With their emphasis on the Eucharist, their

---

[22] *Decree on Ecumenism*, no. 16, in Walter M. Abbott, (ed.) *The Documents of Vatican Council II*, (New York: America Press, 1966), pp. 359-60.

episcopal structure, and their esteem of a synodical government which respects the autonomy of the local church, the Orthodox churches have both the disposition and the institutional structure to participate in such a universal communion. But there are still several problems. First, the Orthodox have generally been uncomfortable with the parallel jurisdictions resulting from the presence in their midst of the Eastern rite Catholic churches. Secondly, there remains the question of how the Protestant churches could be incorporated into the communion of churches.

In respect to the question of parallel jurisdictions, Fr. Pierre Duprey, secretary of the Secretariat for Promoting Christian Unity, has suggested that as an intermediate step on the long road to the ideal of one bishop in a single place, the local church might find its unity through a local episcopal college or council.[23] He points to Beirut—a city which presently has some ten different archbishops or patriarchs, if the Latin rite bishop and the various Eastern rite Catholic and Orthodox bishops are counted together-as a concrete example.

What about the Reformation churches? A solution within the framework of the communion of churches model might be to integrate the Protestant churches as distinct, particular churches, each with its own tradition, spirituality, liturgy, and government, into a universal communion which would then be both larger and more inclusive than the worldwide Roman Catholic Church. Several examples which might serve as models for such a more inclusive communion already exist. One is the ancient church of the first millennium. The inclusion of the Eastern rite Catholic churches within the worldwide Catholic Church is a second. Another, perhaps more appropriate, case is represented by the way Catholicism has been able to accommodate diversity in charism, spirituality, and mission by including within itself the different religious orders and congregations, many of which are themselves presbyteral communities integrated with the episcopal structure of the church.[24]

---

[23]Pierre Duprey, "The Unity We Seek," *Mid-Stream* 17 (1978) 384.

[24]Duprey makes this point, p. 381.

The suggestion that a particular Protestant church might be understood as an order or community within the church rather than as a separate church is not new. Lutheranism began as a reform movement within the universal church and over the years a number of Methodist scholars have noted the similarities between Methodism and a religious order.[25] Communities such as the Quakers and the Salvation Army could also be imagined as lay-administered communities, distinguished by their own spiritualities, within the church catholic, though they would have to have the desire to find a home there and to participate in the church's worship and sacraments.

In order to incorporate the Reformation churches into a universal communion through the analogy with the religious orders, a number of issues would need to be faced.

First, the different churches would have to reach a basic consensus in faith, particularly in regard to those ecclesiological questions which have continued to divide them. That consensus has already emerged to a considerable degree through the various bilateral dialogues and agreed statements, as we have seen. The 1982 World Council of Churches' Lima text, *Baptism, Eucharist and Ministry* (BEM) holds great promise for expressing a consensus which could join the Orthodox, Protestant, and Roman Catholic churches on these issues.[26]

Second, the independence, identities, and theological traditions of the Protestant "particular" churches would have to be respected. Consensus in faith can coexist with different theological traditions and a particular church entering into communion would require an ability to regulate its own affairs greater than that currently enjoyed by Catholic religious orders.

Third, some way must be found to represent the particular churches at the regional and especially the universal church level. In their book Fries and Rahner suggest that all the

---

[25]See for example Geoffrey Wainwright, *The Ecumenical Movement: Crisis and Opportunity for the Church* (Grand Rapids: William B. Eerdmans, 1983), pp. 196-97.

[26]*Baptism, Eucharist and Ministry* (Geneva: WCC, 1982).

particular churches have bishops at the heads of their larger subdivisions.[27] BEM had earlier advanced a similar argument for the recovery of episcopal succession and thus of the historic episcopate in those churches from which it is lacking. BEM regards the episcopal succession "as a sign, though not a guarantee, of the continuity and unity of the Church" (M no. 38). *The COCU Consensus* has adopted a similar position (no. 48).

In tomorrow's church, an office exercising the episcopal function, entered with the participation of bishops in the episcopal succession, would both express the link between the particular church and the ancient church while at the same time such a ministry of unity over the local congregations could represent the regional or particular church within the communion of the world church. Those exercising this office, elected by their respective churches, might even someday take part in the election of the bishop whose ministry involves watching over and expressing the unity of all the churches in the communion, the bishop of Rome. Such a move would not be entirely without precedent, for in the past the various religious orders had cardinal protectors who voted in papal elections.

Conclusions

What can we learn from the different models? In regard to the model of organic union, it is not realistic to imagine the church of tomorrow as a single, organically unified institution. But the model does illustrate the ideal of a community of faith united in sacramental life and mission throughout the world and linked with the apostolic church through visible, institutional bonds.

The model of conciliar fellowship underlines the importance of unity at the local level, and it mediates well between the extremes of the organic union and the reconciled diversity models. On the other hand, achieving organic union for the local church—at least in the foreseeable future—may require

[27]Fries and Rahner, *Unity of the Churches*, pp. 93 ff.

more than what the confessionally or structurally distinct churches are able to offer.

An emphasis on reconciled diversity makes concrete the principle that unity does not mean uniformity, but it runs the risk of permitting such a degree of doctrinal and structural variance that the result would be a reconciliation in name only.

The communion of churches model seems to provide the best way to integrate regional and confessional churches with a worldwide communion such as the Roman Catholic Church. The result would be a more inclusive world church in which particular churches, whether Orthodox or Protestant, could preserve their independence and identity and still participate both liturgically and through their representative leaders in making decisions affecting all Christians.

There still remains the question of the papacy and the role it might play in the church of tomorrow. We shall return to this question in the next chapter.

7

Authority in Tomorrow's Church

The Second Vatican Council spoke of the church as "a kind of sacrament or sign of intimate union with God, and of the unity of all mankind."[1] If the church is to be that sacramental sign of unity in a deeply divided world, it will have to more adequately express within itself that unity for which Christ prayed (John 17:21). Unity is the gift of the Spirit. It cannot be achieved by the churches themselves. On the other hand, the blindness and obstinacy of Christians and their churches can impede the work of the Spirit.

Today the ecumenical movement is testimony to the power and presence of the Spirit. Churches which only thirty years ago still spoke of each other in the polemical language of the sixteenth century are now in the third decade of dialogue. From the dialogues themselves a growing consensus on those issues which had previously divided the churches has emerged. As it continues to grow, the question of unity becomes even more urgent. One of the most divisive issues has been that of authority, and it remains a difficult question. But as we have seen in the preceding chapters, even on this issue a considerable consensus has begun to emerge. It remains partial, for not all the churches subscribe as yet to the ecumenical movement. Some continue to fear it, even to reject the reconciliation and communion which is its goal.

But it is already possible to reach some general conclusions

---

[1] *Dogmatic Constitution on the Church* (LG), no. 1 in *The Documents of Vatican II*, ed. Walter M. Abbott (New York: America Press, 1966), p. 15.

on the question of authority and its exercise in the church of tomorrow. Tomorrow's church will be an ordered church. It will have an authority that is collegial in its structure and in its exercise. Because the church is essentially a *koinonia* or communion of all the baptized, there is a responsibility for the church's life which is shared by all. And finally, there will be a renewed primatial ministry in service of the church's unity. In considering each of these, it may be possible to sketch—though in admittedly broad strokes—what that church might look like.

An Ordered Church

The church of tomorrow must find a way to combine both an authoritative ministry rooted in Catholicism's emphasis on the importance of the church's apostolic office together with a clear recognition of the multiple and diverse nature of the charismatic gifts so valued by Protestantism. Neither hierarchical domination nor an unregulated charismatic " free-for-all" properly describes what the church should be. The church is a differentiated community within which office and charism are related to each other dialectically. Office is rooted in charism which must be discerned before the office is bestowed. One of the important roles of church office is to encourage and regulate the charisms. On the other hand, the multiplicity of charisms continues to challenge office and institution. Those decisions of office holders which are not consistent with the sense of the whole church will not ulti- mately be received and bear fruit in the church's life.

Therefore the ordered or ordained ministry will continue to play an essential role among the many gifts and ministries entrusted to the church. Priests and pastors are authorized to preach the word, preside at the Eucharist, administer the other sacraments in the name of church, and to watch over the church's life. Since many churches already admit both men and women, married and celibate, to the church's or- dained ministry, it seems clear that in the church of tomorrow this ministry will not be restricted on the basis of sex or marital status, even if an individual church may continue to

define the qualifications for this pastoral office more narrowly.

There is no theological reason why those who demonstrate
a charism for leadership in word and worship in local or
basic Christian communities should not be authorized by
church leaders to carry out these roles for their particular
communities, especially when professionally trained priests
or pastors are not available. In Africa many local church
communities are pastored by trained catechists who instruct
candidates, prepare adults for the sacraments, preach the
word and distribute the Eucharist at Sunday worship services. The proposal has been made that these catechists who
are functioning as local pastoral leaders be ordained as auxiliary priests.[2]

Karl Rahner has suggested that in cases such as these the
church might recover the ancient practice of "relative" ordination, that is, authorizing a particular minister with a demonstrated charism for leadership to function as priest within the
context of a particular local community.[3] But what will remain necessary is that those to be authorized to preach and
preside in the name of the church be received into this collegial ministry by the laying on of hands by those who already
exercise this office. In this way the new minister's communion
and that of the minister's community with the apostolic and
universal church can be made visible.

Though it would be difficult to maintain that a Protestant
church would have to adopt the traditional threefold structure of the ordained ministry, in the ecumenical dialogues
there is a growing consensus on the value of this ministry of
bishops, presbyters, and deacons as a structure which might
be incorporated for the sake of unity.

In particular, a consensus is growing on the importance of
the episcopal office in communion with the historic episcopate. Without implying that churches not in the historic
succession through the episcopal office do not have authentic

[2]Raymond Hickey, *A Case for an Auxiliary Priesthood* (Maryknoll, New York:
Orbis Books, 1982).

[3]Karl Rahner, *The Shape of the Church to Come*, (New York: Seabury Press,
1974), p. 110.

ministries, there is a growing sense that this historic episcopal office and succession should be recovered. Episcopal succession functions as a sign of continuity with the apostolic church while the episcopal office itself provides a means of entering into communion and decision-making responsibility with the worldwide communion of churches. At the same time there is a growing recognition that the episcopal office and the threefold ministry in general stand in need of considerable reform.

There is not yet a clear consensus on teaching authority, but a growing number of churches are coming to recognize that a responsibility for guarding and teaching the apostolic faith both corporately and individually belongs to the office of bishop. The church of tomorrow will need an effective teaching office to proclaim the faith of the church with a clear voice. Too often when this authority has been absent the unity of the church has suffered further disintegration.

At the same time the real context of this teaching office is the liturgical preaching of the word of God which belongs to the bishop as the one who presides over the life of the community and finds consensus after the word has been proclaimed, reflected upon, and prayed over in the concrete circumstances of the community's life. When the teaching office is removed from its original liturgical and kerygmatic context it loses much of its credibility and risks being perceived merely as part of the church's administrative bureaucracy. Therefore a renewed threefold ministry should also provide for a teaching office rooted in pastoral responsibility for the local church and joined in a collegial relationship with the worldwide episcopacy.

A Collegial Authority

The term collegiality has been used to describe the shared responsibility of the bishops and pope for the government of the universal church, most clearly seen in an ecumenical council.[4] The concept of collegiality emerged in the patristic

[4]Charles M. Murphy, "Collegiality: An Essay Toward Better Understanding," *Theological Studies* 46 (1985) 38-49.

period when the Latin word *collegium* or college was used to designate the *ordo* or body of the bishops.[5] But the term did not assume its present prominence in the vocabulary of Roman Catholics until after the Second Vatican Council. The Council, in developing the theology of the episcopal office, stressed that the bishops who are united to each other and to the pope through hierarchical communion constitute a college or body.[6] Vatican II's collegial approach to church authority was in marked contrast to the monarchical approach of Vatican I and pre-Vatican II Catholicism in general.

In describing episcopal collegiality Patrick Granfield singles out three principles which are implied in the concept.[7] First, collegiality is primarily a theological reality rather than a juridical structure. It is rooted in the *communio [koinonia]* of the church which joins believers together through faith, grace, and the Holy Spirit, and is made visible in the Eucharist. Episcopal authority is not derived from the pope; like collegiality itself, it is sacramental, rooted in the sacrament of orders.[8]

Second, episcopal collegiality is dependent on the pope who is the head of the episcopal college. According to *Lumen gentium* the power of the episcopal order "can be exercised only with the consent of the Roman Pontiff."[9]

Third, collegiality is essentially dialogic. It requires careful listening, honest exchange of views, and the willingness to work toward consensus. But this is true not only of episcopal collegiality; this dialogic principle should characterize the exercise of authority on all levels of the church.

It is probably true that collegiality is more effective in the Roman Catholic Church today on the level of national

---

[5]Joseph Ratzinger, "The Pastoral Implications of Episcopal Collegiality," in Edward Schillebeeckx, (ed.), *The Church and Mankind*, (Concilium Vol. 1) (Glen Rock, NJ: Paulist Press, 1965), pp. 47-50.

[6]LG no. 22, Abbott, pp. 42-43.

[7]Patrick Granfield, *The Limits of the Papacy* (New York: Crossroad, 1987) pp. 82-87.

[8]See LG no. 27.

[9]LG no. 25, Abbott 43.

episcopal conferences than it is on the level of the universal church. The national and regional conferences of bishops which have developed since Vatican II have given Catholic bishops throughout the church a new familiarity with a collegial exercise of authority. Some episcopal conferences have become particularly effective instruments for teaching and church renewal. The Episcopal Conference of Latin America (CELAM), especially through its meetings at Medellín (1968) and Puebla (1979), has played an important role in the renewal of the Catholic Church throughout Latin America. And the National Conference of Catholic Bishops (NCCB) has emerged as one of the most progressive on social issues. The recent pastoral letters of the American bishops on peace and on the economy,[10] formulated through a broadly consultative process over a period of several years, have been widely read and discussed.

The precise theological basis of episcopal conferences and the nature of their authority is still being debated.[11] Cardinal Joseph Ratzinger has argued that episcopal conferences do not belong to the structure of the church, and hence, have no theological basis.[12] Avery Dulles agrees that they are not formally authorized by divine law, but he holds that as structures organized by the bishops in order to carry out their mission, like other ecclesiastical structures, "they have real authority based on the divinely established order of the Church."[13]

Tomorrow's church must find a way to incorporate Protestant and Orthodox churches into a worldwide communion of churches diverse in theological traditions, liturgies, and

---

[10] *The Challenge of Peace: God's Promise and Our Response* (Washington: USCC, 1983) and *Economic Justice for All: Pastoral Letter on Catholic Social Teaching* (Washington: USCC, 1986).

[11] See Granfield, *The Limits of the Papacy*, pp. 98-100.

[12] Joseph Cardinal Ratzinger, with Vitterio Messori, *The Ratzinger Report* (San Francisco: Ignatius Press, 1985), p. 60.

[13] Avery Dulles, "Bishops' Conference Documents: What Doctrinal Authority?" *Origins* 14 (1985) 530. See also the articles by Dulles, James H. Provost, Ladislas Orsy, and Joseph A. Komonchak reacting to the preliminary draft of the Vatican working paper on the theological and juridical status of episcopal conferences, published in *America* 158 (1988).

government, united in faith, and able to participate through their representative leaders in collegially making decisions affecting all Christians.

A Shared Responsibility

We noted earlier that both the WCC *Baptism, Ministry and Eucharist* text and *The COCU Consensus* see considerable advantages in the traditional threefold ministry, while at the same time expecting it to be reformed so that it might function in a more personal, collegial and communal way.[14] In speaking of a communal dimension to the way ordained ministry is exercised, BEM points to "the intimate relationship between the ordained ministry and the community," and consequently, the need to provide for "the community's effective participation in the discovery of God's will and the guidance of the Spirit" (M no. 26). Adequate expression of the personal, collegial, and communal dimension of ministry should allow "the active participation of all members in the life and the decision-making of the community" (M no. 27). *The COCU Consensus* goes even further. In a departure from traditional usage which underlines a congregationalist orientation, the COCU document expands BEM's concept of collegiality beyond its reference to the college of ordained ministers. It is understood as describing a "shared responsibility" and "partnership in governance" which includes both clergy and laity (*COCU Consensus* no. 22b).

The Roman Catholic Church, with its hierarchical orientation and its insistence that the common priesthood of the faithful and the hierarchical priesthood "differ from one another in essence and not only in degree,"[15] has found it difficult to provide room in its theory and practice for participation by the non-ordained in decision-making as well as in the formulation of church teaching.

Today, however, a number of Catholic theologians are

---

[14]See above, p. 100.

[15]LG no. 10, Abbott p. 27.

emphasizing baptism as the sacramental foundation of all ministry. It is baptism which constitutes the church as a *koinonia* or communion. These theologians look to Vatican II's emphasis on the church as the People of God and emphasize charism, competence, and collegiality over ordination, office, and hierarchy.[16] We described this earlier as a charismatic model of authority.[17]

But is the church fundamentally an institution, exercising authority from the top down, or is it fundamentally a community in which all the members are mutually dependent even in the exercise of authority? Or in other words, does the hierarchy have a sacred power which enables it to function independently of the church or is there a mutuality or interdependence which exists between all members of the church and which implies a shared responsibility between ordained and non-ordained? The traditional doctrine of the *sensus fidelium* or sense of the faithful[18] and the ecclesial reality of reception both imply an interdependence of teaching authority and the body of the faithful. Now a recent study of the way the papal magisterium has functioned in the Catholic Church by J. Robert Dionne suggests that there is an element of interdependence in the church's very nature.[19]

Basically Dionne argues that the Catholic Church's theory on the way authority is exercised is not really in agreement with the church's praxis. The crux of the problem may be seen in the constitution *Pastor aeternus* of Vatican I (1870) which proclaimed the dogma of papal infallibility. The constitution states that *ex cathedra* definitions are "irreformable of themselves [*ex sese*], and not from the consent of the Church" (DS 3074). Dionne holds that the *ex sese* clause means "that in exercising the extraordinary magisterium the Roman Bishop does not need *in any strict or absolute sense*

[16]See for example John A Coleman, "The Future of Ministry," *America* 144 (1981) 243-49.

[17]See above, pp. 32-36.

[18]See J.M.R. Tillard, "*Sensus Fidelium,*" *One in Christ* 11 (1975) 2-29; Avery Dulles, "*Sensus Fidelium,*" *America* 155 (1986) 240-42; 263.

[19]J. Robert Dionne, *The Papacy and the Church: A Study of Praxis and Reception in Ecumenical Perspective* (New York: Philosophical Library, 1987).

the prior or subsequent agreement of the rest of the Catholic Church."[20] Does this mean that the papal magisterium is self-sufficient, that it functions independently of the faith of the entire church?

Dionne shows conclusively that the answer to this question is "no." He analyzes the exercise of both the ordinary and the extraordinary papal magisterium, illustrating that in both cases papal teaching has been influenced by or exercised in a dialogue with the church. First, he shows how some consistent teachings of Piux IX and his successors were ultimately modified or reversed by the Second Vatican Council because of the "modalities" of their reception, or more specifically, as a result of the "appropriate criticism" and "talking back" to Rome on the part of theologians.[21] Second, he shows that when the extraordinary papal magisterium was exercised in the definitions of the Immaculate Conception (1854) and Assumption (1950) of Mary, the proclamations were not made without the consent of the church, for both definitions were made only after a process of consulting the church through a polling of the bishops.

As a result of his analysis Dionne argues that the church cannot be understood simply as an institution, for it involves what he calls "associative elements"—that is, elements of mutual dependence—even on the level of doctrine and dogma.[22] That associative elements or elements of mutual dependence enter into the articulation of doctrine is clear from his study of those cases where the teaching of the ordinary papal magisterium was modified or reversed because of critical modes of reception on the part of theologians. On this level he goes so far as to suggest that ordinary papal teachings may be judged to be without error only when they have been so received by the rest of the church.[23] More

[20]Ibid., p. 302; Dionne seems to be stressing the ontological priority of an infallible statement. Others would argue that the *ex sese* clause means only that *ex cathedra* definitions do not need subsequent juridical validation by a higher tribunal; see J.M.R. Tillard, *The Bishop of Rome* (Wilmington, DE: Michael Glazier, 1983), pp. 174-176.

[21]Dionne, *The Papacy and the Church*, pp. 83-236; see above p. 107.

[22]Ibid., p. 297.

[23]Ibid., p. 357.

significant perhaps is his conclusion after studying the process which led to the two *ex cathedra* definitions: "even on the level of the extraordinary papal magisterium, *Church as association* was intimately involved with *Church as institution.*"[24]

At this point there are similarities between Dionne's ecclesiology and that of Leonardo Boff. Dionne suggests that the distinction between the *ecclesia docens* [teaching church] and the *ecclesia discens* [learning church] may not be as clear-cut as previously supposed.[25] Boff argues that *docens* and *discens* are two functions of one community; they cannot be understood as two parts or divisions within the church.[26]

Dionne's study is significant because it shows that even in the exercising of doctrinal authority the church functions as a *koinonia* or communion. This vision of church represents a differentiated ecclesiology, a middle ground between a strictly hierarchical or institutional ecclesiology and a congregationalist or egalitarian ecclesiology with no provision for an episcopal teaching office. Dionne concludes by suggesting that a revision of church theory on the basis of church praxis could lead to an ecumenical breakthrough. But one can draw a further implication. If the church involves an element of interdependence or shared responsibility in its very nature, then finding ways to better express this in the church's government by involving the non-ordained in significant ways would not be contrary to the church's essential nature.

Incorporating a more participatory style for the exercise of authority in the Roman Catholic Church will depend in large measure on a renewed papal ministry.

[24]Ibid., p. 336; italics in original.

[25]Ibid., 349.

[26]Leonardo Boff, *Church: Charism and Power*, (New York: Crossroad, 1985) pp. 138-139.

A Renewed Primacy

The final issue regarding authority in the church of tomorrow concerns the role of the papacy. Roman Catholics believe that one of the contributions of the Catholic tradition to tomorrow's church is the ministry of unity exercised historically by the bishop of Rome. In their book, *Unity of the Churches*, Heinrich Fries and Karl Rahner presuppose that the time has come for the major church traditions or particular churches to accept this office.[27] And indeed, the importance of the Petrine ministry for tomorrow's church is acknowledged by a number of ecumenists and ecumenical dialogues, as we have already seen.

But it is important not to overlook a caution raised by the late Willem Visser't Hooft, considered to be the founding father of the World Council of Churches. In an article written shortly before his death, Visser't Hooft warned:

> Those non-Roman churches which might be willing to concede that a united church could have a Petrine office are not saying loudly enough that in their view this office would in several respects be fundamentally different from the papacy as it exists today. The unifying ministry which they have in mind is not the authoritarian, centralized universal jurisdiction as defined in 1870, or in the *Codex Juris Canonici.*[28]

Catholic theologians are aware of this also. Visser't Hooft quotes with approval Yves Congar's summary of the attitude towards the papacy which has developed through the ecumenical movement: "A papacy such as history has made it—centralizing, imperial, narrowly authoritarian: no! A papal ministry presiding over the communion and the unity

---

[27]Heinrich Fries and Karl Rahner, *Unity of the Churches: A Real Possibility* (New York/Philadelphia: Paulist Press/Fortress Press, 1985), p. ix.

[28]W.A. Visser't Hooft, "WCC-Roman Catholic Relations: Some Personal Reflections," *The Ecumenical Review* 37 (1985) 338; see, for example, all the rights and powers which Granfield lists as belonging to the pope according to the new Code of Canon Law; *The Papacy and the Church*, pp. 44-50.

in a collegial and conciliar system: why not?"[29] This new attitude towards the papacy on the part of so many Protestants presents a very real challenge to the leadership of the Roman Catholic Church.

As more interest is expressed in the Petrine ministry on the part of Protestant Christians, it will become increasingly necessary for the Roman Catholic Church to develop a more pastoral, truly collegial style of leadership for this unique ministry which is to serve the visible unity of the church. For Roman Catholics the Petrine office is a matter of dogma. At the same time, the development of the papacy has been influenced by social, cultural, and political factors that are not identical with the dogmatic nature of the Petrine ministry and which can frustrate the very purpose it is intended to serve. Therefore we need to ask, what can be separated out as historically or culturally conditioned accidents from the essential nature of the papacy. In what follows, I will try to suggest some ways in which the exercise of authority might be changed and the papal primacy renewed in the Roman Catholic Church, in order to better express the collegiality and shared responsibility which must find expression in the church of tomorrow.

1. A More Participatory Style of Decision-Making. Roman Catholic teaching assigns to the college of bishops in union with its head, the bishop of Rome, "supreme and full power over the universal Church."[30] Each bishop also exercises over his own church power which is "proper, ordinary, and immediate, although its exercise is ultimately regulated by the supreme authority of the Church and can be circumscribed by certain limits, for the advantage of the Church or of the faithful."[31] Without taking anything away theologically from the leadership role of the bishop of Rome or episcopal college, it would be possible for the Roman Catholic Church to develop a more participatory style of government, involving wider consultation and representation of the laity.

[29]Ibid; see Yves Congar, *Essais oecumeniques* (Paris: Centurion, 1984), p. 93.

[30]LG no. 22, Abbott p. 43.

[31]Ibid., no. 37; Abbott p. 51.

Certainly the synodal form of government of the churches of the Anglican Communion which allows clergy and laity to participate along with with the bishops in decision-making presents no obstacle to eventual reconciliation between that Communion and the Roman Catholic Church. Without diminishing the importance of the episcopal or papal office, the Roman Catholic Church could learn much from those churches with synodal structures of government.

2. *Broader Participation in the Formulation of Church Teaching.* The process used in formulating the recent pastoral letters of the American Catholic bishops on peace and the U. S. economy provides a concrete example of broad consultation involving theologians, recognized scholars, and representatives of government, even if this process is not always admired in Rome. We saw earlier that in the Middle Ages and even later representatives from the various orders in the church, including the university doctors of sacred theology, have participated in the church's councils.[32] So there is a precedent for broadening the way that the church's teaching magisterium might be exercised in the church of tomorrow.

One of the more positive aspects of the 1987 Synod of Bishops on the Laity was the participation of the theological experts and lay auditors with the bishops in the small group discussions. Is there any reason why this kind of participation by theologians and representatives of the laity could not become a regular feature of future episcopal synods? Pope John Paul II's words at the synod's closing liturgy were encouraging. He expressed gratitude for the participation of the lay men and women and said: "In a certain sense, the experience of this synod is unprecedented; and hopefully it will become a 'model,' a reference point for the future."[33]

3. *The Selection of Bishops.* The question of how bishops are selected is a critical one. In the ancient church bishops were selected by local churches; often the custom was to inform the bishop of Rome subsequently so that he might

---

[32]See above, pp. 67-69.

[33]John Paul II, "The Pope's Closing Synod Homily," *Origins* 17 (1987) 390.

recognize the new bishop. In this way the visible communion between the local churches and the bishop of Rome which constituted the church catholic was both expressed and maintained.

Only in the nineteenth century did the popes begin to actually choose bishops throughout the world. But even in very recent history secular governments have had considerable say in the process. Candidates for the episcopacy in Spain were subject to veto by the Spanish dictator, General Francisco Franco. The governments of France, Austria, West Germany, Ecuador, Portugal, Dominican Republic, Poland, Venezuela, Argentina, El Salvador, and Colombia are recognized as having the *droit de regard* or right to consultation, enabling a state to make known any objections it might have to a candidate for the episcopal office.[34] If the church historically has made this kind of accommodation with governments, even repressive ones, there is no reason why it could not grant the right to local churches to name their own bishops, with the understanding that they would have to be recognized by the Apostolic See in Rome in order to be in communion with the universal church. The dioceses or local churches of Basel and St. Gallen in Switzerland still exercise this right. The new Code of Canon Law (1983) states that the pope "freely appoints Bishops or confirms those lawfully elected" (can. 375). Certainly in any future union, non-Roman Catholic churches would have to preserve the right to name their own episcopal authorities.

4. *Episcopal Collegiality.* The relation between the head and members of the episcopal college has seen different expressions, reflecting the social and political forms of different historical periods. After some six centuries in which authority was increasingly centralized in the papacy and understood juridically, the Roman Catholic Church since Vatican II has been moving in the direction of a more collegial form of government. Thanks largely to Pope Paul VI's establishment of the Synod of Bishops, the structure for a more collegial exercise of church authority is already in place, though it is

[34]See Granfield, *The Limits of the Papacy,* p. 76.

not clear that the synod is presently functioning in a truly collegial manner. True collegiality in the Roman Catholic Church will be realized not just when the representatives of the bishops of the world gather every three years or so in Rome, but when the bishops themselves have more to say in the determination of what is placed on the synod's agenda. They should also have more say over what will be included in the synod's final report.

The question of a truly ecumenical council in the future which would include representatives of all the Christian churches (or of all those interested in attending) poses a further problem. From a Protestant perspective, J. Robert Nelson has pointed out that the role of the pope at such an event "will have to be one which is representative of, and subordinate to, the universal council."[35] This raises again the conciliarist doctrine of the supremacy of a general assembly of bishops over a pope, proclaimed by the Council of Constance in the decree *Haec sancta* (1415) but not received by the Catholic Church. However the precise meaning and status of this decree is still debated.

Others have suggested a voluntary limitation of those powers and rights which Catholic doctrine and church law accord to the pope.[36] In a sense, this would amount to a voluntary "constitutionalizing" of papal authority. At the same time, care must be taken not to deprive the pope of the ability to act which his role as chief pastor demands. A spirit of collegiality on the part of all who exercise authority is more important than laws and canons. As Patrick Granfield has written, "In the final analysis collegiality cannot be satisfactorily realized by legal prescriptions."[37]

5. *Teaching Authority and Infallibility.* The dogma of infallibility remains one of the most complex issues to resolve, though it is not often properly understood by either

---

[35]J. Robert Nelson, "Methodism and the Papacy," in *A Pope for All Christians*, ed. Peter J. McCord (New York: Paulist Press, 1976), p. 172.

[36]See Karl Rahner, "Open Questions in Dogma Considered by the Institutional Church as Definitely Answered," *Journal of Ecumenical Studies* 15 (1978) 219-220; Granfield, *The Limits of the Papacy*, pp. 183-188.

[37]Granfield, *The Limits of the Papacy*, p. 188.

Protestants or Roman Catholics. Dogmatically, infallibility is basically a statement about the faith of the whole church which comes to official expression when a pope or council teaches *ex cathedra*, that is, explicitly and with full authority. Infallibility is a charism entrusted to the whole church; it does not belong to the pope alone. Infallibility is limited, both in its exercise and in the definitions themselves which are conditioned by the knowledge, concerns, thought categories, and language of any given historical period.

Karl Rahner pointed out shortly before his death that while an increasing number of Protestant ecumenists are willing to recognize a Petrine ministry exercised by the bishop of Rome in the church of the future, still many have considerable hesitations on this subject of papal teaching authority. They fear that acknowledging a Roman teaching primacy would mean "signing a blank check" which could lead some day to new problems.[38] In response to this concern Rahner has made a number of observations. First, he states that since it is clear conciliar doctrine that *ex cathedra* definitions do not involve introducing new revelation, it is evident that in order to exercise the teaching function today there is a moral obligation to conduct some sort of inquiry at least among the bishops worldwide. Second, he suggests that if the pope was to exercise this infallible teaching authority in the future, it would probably involve a new expression of the fundamental substance of Christianity rather than the further material differentiation of that substance, as for example, the Marian dogmas of Pius IX and Pius XII represented. If the infallible papal magisterium was to be exercised at all, it would probably be used only to defend the faith and re-express it in more contemporary language.[39]

Rahner also suggests that the papal teaching authority might seek to safeguard the religious conscience of non-Catholic Christians by presenting its teaching as "authentic and nondefining declarations," without the added step of

[38]Karl Rahner, in Rahner and Fries, *Unity of the Churches*, p. 87; see also his "Open Questions," p. 220.

[39]Rahner, "Open Questions," pp. 222-223; see also *Unity of the Churches*, pp. 88-89.

regarding them as demanding an obedience of faith. Finally, it would be possible to provide a way for the various partner churches in any future union to participate in the exercise of that authority, perhaps through a restructuring of the Congregation for the Doctrine of the Faith.[40]

6. *Participation in Papal Elections.* Some years ago the suggestion was made that the papacy might be a rotating office, held for a limited term by representatives of the different churches. Thus a Roman Catholic bishop might hold the office for five years, to be followed by the President of the Southern Baptist Convention for five years, and then by the General Secretary of the World Council of Churches. But this is unrealistic. The emergence of the Petrine ministry or papacy cannot be separated from the primacy of the Roman church itself. Already in the second century Rome's unique authority was recognized on the basis of its unique apostolic heritage; the church of Rome claimed not just one but two founding apostles, both Peter and Paul. There is evidence of the church of Rome instructing other churches as early as the New Testament period. In the 80s the first letter of Peter was sent from Rome in Peter's name to a group of Christians in Asia Minor. And 1 Clement was sent from Rome to admonish the church of Corinth around the year 96.[41]

More practically, if the church of tomorrow is to be understood as a communion of churches, provisions could be made for representatives of the various regional or particular churches to participate in the election of the bishop of Rome. The present method of electing a new pope—through an assembly or conclave of the College of Cardinals—is a matter of human law and could be either expanded or changed, to better accommodate the new circumstances of a wider communion of churches presided over by the bishop of Rome.

[40]Rahner, *Unity of the Churches*, pp. 90-91.

[41]See Thomas P. Rausch, *The Roots of the Catholic Tradition* (Wilmington, DE: Michael Glazier, 1986), pp. 163-166.

Conclusions

We have seen that authority is as necessary in the church as it is in other institutions, but also that its fundamental inspiration is different. In the Christian community all authority must be modeled on the example of Jesus who saw his own role as that of a servant for the sake of the reign of God. An effective authority, finding its example in the authority of Jesus, will be just as important in the church of tomorrow.

Tomorrow's church hopefully will be both more pluralistic and more universal than the church of today. In such a church there will need to be a rich diversity of ministries both ordained and non-ordained. Neither office nor charism can be subsumed into the other. The charismatic element must always be recognized and allowed to flourish in communities linked with the church catholic and apostolic through its ordained ministers.

The church of tomorrow will continue to reflect more deeply on the implications of baptism, which calls all Christians to a shared responsibility for the life of the community and to a participation in decisions affecting its mission. It will more clearly reflect the mutuality and interdependence of all members which is rooted in the very nature of the church as a *koinonia* or communion of disciples.

Tomorrow's church should integrate Protestant and Orthodox churches into the worldwide communion of the Roman Catholic Church in such a way that a more inclusive communion of churches results. It will be a church at once catholic and reformed. It will have a collegial authority exercising the episcopal function and teaching office. This office must be capable of representing the different churches in conciliar assemblies on the regional or world level and of interpreting the gospel with authority both for the churches themselves and in the context of their societies.

Finally, in such a church, representing a true community of peoples in a divided and suffering world, the ministry of one who will serve and symbolize the unity of the church universal will be especially important. This ministry already exists in the office of the bishop of Rome. Renewed in the light of the gospel and attentive to the concerns of all Christians, it could be one of Catholicism's most significant contributions to the church of tomorrow.

Subject Index

Index of Authors

157